Praise for *Meaning Train*

"What our deeply divided world needs is a fresh and welcoming approach to connection with others. Carrie Cunningham's talent is opening doors and inviting us to accompany her as she encounters fascinating people and places. Along the way, we gather the context that helps us understand the beloved community that our world so desperately needs. Carrie's love of stories—from personal narratives to great books—rubs off on us as we travel through these pages. When you finish her book, you'll want to go out and meet new people and read some of the books she recommends. This book is an invitation to an ongoing adventure."

—David Crumm, editor of *ReadTheSpirit* magazine

Meaning Train

Essays on Religion and Politics

Carrie Cunningham

This book is a work of non-fiction. Unless otherwise noted, the author and the publisher make no explicit guarantees as to the accuracy of the information contained in this book and in some cases, names of people and places have been altered to protect their privacy.

Archway Publishing books may be ordered through booksellers or by contacting:

Archway Publishing
1663 Liberty Drive
Bloomington, IN 47403
www.archwaypublishing.com
1 (888) 242-5904

Because of the dynamic nature of the Internet, any web addresses or links contained in this book may have changed since publication and may no longer be valid. The views expressed in this work are solely those of the author and do not necessarily reflect the views of the publisher, and the publisher hereby disclaims any responsibility for them.

Any people depicted in stock imagery provided by Getty Images are models, and such images are being used for illustrative purposes only. Certain stock imagery © Getty Images.

All Scripture quotations are taken from the King James Version.

ISBN: 978-1-4808-7881-5 (sc)
ISBN: 978-1-4808-7882-2 (e)

Library of Congress Control Number: 2019906768

Print information available on the last page.

Archway Publishing rev. date: 06/18/2019

You don't choose your family. They are God's
gift to you are as you are to them.

—Desmond Tutu

Never throw food away when you are near the poor,
for you are an ambassador of God on earth.

—Bamgambiki Habyarimanna

For Lar Bear, MoMo and my family.

Introduction

Meaning Train is the result of a decades-long immersion in human rights. I have reached a point in my life where my principles are sacrosanct and my hopes are secure. I am a progressive Christian, and through my writing, I aim to illuminate how religion can be a force for good. I believe the politically and economically distressed can find equality and economic freedom through the nonviolent and loving tenets of most religions. For me, the answer to human struggle is Christianity. I yearn to build societies based on Jesus's example. His insight to love everyone was revolutionary for the world.

The inspiration for *Meaning Train* is the notion of beloved community. Created and embraced by the 1960s civil rights leaders, the concept calls for solving human rights issues via nonviolence coupled with radical love and forgiveness. Based on the example of Jesus Christ, the notion guided leaders like Martin Luther King Jr. in addition to John Lewis and Fanny Lou Hammer. Together, with love and care in their hearts, they ended the segregation laws of Jim Crow and black disenfranchisement. They risked their lives so that people would know the necessity of equality and having a voice. Lewis thought it was like bringing the kingdom of God to earth, while Hammer said it was like a welcoming table where everyone is included in a splendid feast.

"Without prayer, without faith in the Almighty, the Civil Rights Movement would have been a bird without wings," Lewis said.

My route toward becoming an advocate for love and nonviolence has been long and grueling, but also meaningful and rewarding. I grew up in an affluent home in Grosse Pointe Farms, Michigan. My interest in human rights was viscerally grounded in my father's racism and antisemitism. His parents were from the South, and he was influenced by their loathsome views on racial and religious diversity. Still, he had some goodness within him, and he loved our family. I forgive him for his views.

Coming from humble origins, my mom was a saint who gave my siblings and me insatiable love. Her altruism reflected the spirit of beloved community. She dedicated her life to service and philanthropy, raising money for schools and hospitals. My mom taught me the necessity of grace by enduring hardship and caring about the world.

As a student at Harvard College in the 1990s, I valued the growth of my intellectual life. To be sure, it was at Harvard where my interest in human rights began and flourished. I majored in American history and minored in African history. The first class I took with my favorite professor, James Goodman, centered on 1920s and 1930s American history. It changed my life. I learned about how Franklin Roosevelt made some progress on race, and I was introduced to the Southern psychology of white hegemony. This enlightenment about race in America revealed the potential source of my father's vitriol. Moreover, it nurtured my nascent voice on civil rights. My work on apartheid for African history classes was equally meaningful.

When my mom died of breast cancer in 2000, I became a Christian. I was previously an atheist and unaware of how faith can engender meaning and hope. Upset about my mom's death and also dispirited and frightened about a violent world, I found solace in the majesty of Jesus. Later, at Wayne State University, I learned about other religions like Judaism and Islam as I worked toward another bachelor's degree in Near Eastern Studies. This religious journey gave me a new sense of purpose to help the world via nonviolent and loving principles.

This collection of essays fuses the material I learned at Harvard with my religious education. From an examination of race and love for others in major religions to studies of American heroes like David McCullough and Bobby Kennedy, the book explores the wonder of human existence. Examples of my work in the book include essays about the guiding Christian ethos of John Lewis's activism in addition to themes of inclusion in Judaism and Islam.

For instance, John Lewis held on to the concept of creating a beloved community even as he was beaten by white supremacists. His story is fantastically delineated in his book *Across That Bridge*. The son of a sharecropper, Lewis's nonviolent mission to create racial equality was galvanized by listening to Martin Luther King. Lewis believed that humans were made in God's image to be interconnected and love one another. Bigotry, he thought, maims the white racists us much as the black victims. In Lewis's mind, the civil rights movement would triumph because humans are innately good.

Another essay on the 1991 exodus of Ethiopian Jews to Israel reflects ideals of acceptance. The story is told by Jew Asher Naim in his book *Saving the Lost Tribe*. The Ethiopian Jews were oppressed by the majority Ethiopian Christians. Many lacked homes and needed money and education. They were excluded from food rations because they didn't live in Ethiopia's capital, Addis Ababa. Naim, an Israeli diplomat to Ethiopia, orchestrated their route to Israel with the help of America. He cared about the Ethiopian Jews. Naim's action reveals how Israel helps and makes a home for dispossessed Jews. His actions are noble and exemplary.

A piece about Muslims in America similarly reveals themes of belonging. Denounced by some in the American public domain and by Republicans in the 2016 presidential race in particular, Muslims have endured atrocious discrimination in America, writer Arsalan Iftikhar says in his book *Scapegoats*. Their Prophet Muhammed has been castigated among American politicians and some media outlets.

Moreover, their Sharia law, which includes commentary on the Quran, has been eschewed even though it is good and rich with peaceful virtue. Still, many brave Americans have rejected Islamophobia and have called for tolerance. Just as African Americans, Jews, and Catholics have and continue to battle intolerance in America, so will Muslims. The diverse American mosaic should assure it.

The panoply of essays in this collection should reflect a nonviolent and good moral compass that humans can embrace to make the world a better place. No matter what religion or ethnicity, people can contemplate this compass, and with fortitude and care, we will make the world a more caring and just world.

Part 1

Race

Team of Rivals: How Lincoln Changed American Democracy

Doris Kearns Goodwin's *Team of Rivals*, a mesmerizing account of the presidency of Abraham Lincoln, is an invaluable book for anyone concerned about the experiment called America.

Goodwin is a widely esteemed American biographer and historian whose writing and thinking abilities are exceptional. In addition to *Team of Rivals*, she has written *The Fitzgeralds and the Kennedys: An American Saga, Lyndon Johnson and The American Dream*, and the Pulitzer Prize-winning book *No Ordinary Time: Franklin and Eleanor Roosevelt.*

Goodwin also contributes informed political commentary to NBC News. Her husband, Richard N. Goodwin, worked as an adviser and speech writer for President John F. Kennedy, President Lyndon B. Johnson, and Senator Robert F. Kennedy.

Team of Rivals has been widely discussed as President Barack Obama spoke with Goodwin about her book and has cited it as a guide for creating his cabinet. Moreover, Obama has described Lincoln as one of his heroes who he would like to emulate.

Goodwin's portrait of Lincoln mirrors the ascendant and meaningful story of Obama in many ways. Lincoln is a complex but compelling man. Cool and composed, noble and tender, generous and empathetic, the nation's sixteenth president encountered the task of ending slavery and keeping the Union together.

Goodwin's book shows how Lincoln's temperament enabled him to find solutions to issues by cultivating conversation among his radical and conservative cabinet members. The resulting diverse discourse shaped his stances on the issue of slavery and the Union. And this in turn spurred Lincoln to author the Emancipation Proclamation, a crowning achievement of his presidency and a bulwark for future improvements in American democracy.

The men who Lincoln surrounded himself with included radicals William Seward, a New York senator; and Salmon Chase, an Ohio governor; in addition to conservative Edward Bates, a Missouri statesman. They served as secretary of state, secretary of the treasury, and attorney general respectively. These men consulted Lincoln on many crucial questions, but Lincoln made the final decisions. As Goodwin described, Lincoln shared his opinions but determined results by himself.

The making of Lincoln's opinions on slavery and Union were very intricate, multifaceted, and sometimes contradictory. He vowed to end slavery's expansion in the American territories, but his viewpoints were built by gradual, if forceful, consensus. He often plowed central ground but simultaneously held on to principle even as his ideas changed during his presidency.

The foundation of Lincoln's viewpoints was often based on the words of the Declaration of Independence, which proclaims all men are "equal in 'certain inalienable rights, among which are life, liberty, and the pursuit of happiness.'" He invoked the declaration in his opposition to both the Dred Scott Supreme Court decision, which ruled that blacks were not citizens, and the Kansas-Nebraska Act, which gave citizens there the choice regarding slavery. He was gradually chipping away at slavery.

Building on the Declaration of Independence, Lincoln issued the Emancipation Proclamation, which freed all slaves in January 1863. The drafting of the document, its contents, and its introduction to America reveal the true essence of Lincoln's statesmanship: he was skilled and pragmatic, visionary and principled.

In mid-1862, with America engaged in fighting between Unionists and Secessionists, Lincoln listened to cabinet members argue about slavery and the Union. "While he concurred with abolitionists that slavery was a 'moral, social and political wrong' as president he could not ignore the Constitutional protection of the institution where it already existed," Goodwin wrote.

To circumvent this issue, Lincoln used the constitutional-based war powers of the president to free slaves in rebel states so they could help the Union on the battlefield. Lincoln waited for victory at Antietam before he released a draft to the public. He wanted people in the Union, whose views were constantly moving and changing like his own, to support the proclamation. And they did support the text with a full heart.

The proclamation was primarily a military document, but its symbolism was epochal and potent.

While the Emancipation Proclamation was a historic achievement for Lincoln, he still had disparaging views on race. In a meeting with freed slaves at the White House, he said, "When you cease to be slaves, you are yet far removed from being placed on an equal plane with the white race," adding that on the North American Continent "not a single man of your race is made the equal of a single man of ours."

As part of his view of blacks, he wanted to colonize them in other areas in the world after they were freed.

While these views are dispiriting, Lincoln changed his position over the years. As he came across more blacks and talked with them, he felt more respect for them and jettisoned his ideas of colonization.

All in all, Lincoln remains an American icon and iconoclast. Making momentous decisions about America, he put in place the basis for American ideals of freedom and equality to be realized.

Guiding a war-torn and fragile republic, he helped make America what is it today. It is a place of promise and hope, goodness and optimism. It's a place that elected Obama its first black president.

Desmond Tutu Book Celebrates God's Love

Desmond Tutu is a Nobel Peace Prize laureate who helped expunge South African apartheid and then led his country on a path of forgiveness and healing. He is an empathetic icon who believes the goodness of God resides in everyone.

Tutu was featured on the Detroit, Michigan, religion website *ReadTheSpirit* for good reason. He has written a beautiful book called *Made for Goodness* with his daughter Mpho Tutu. With poetic language, *Made for Goodness* supports the recognition of God's infinite love and guides readers to a life of goodness and meaning. It is a stirring book for all the world.

This book matters as violent conflicts simmer across the world. From Israelis and Palestinians to Iraq and Syria, the Middle East caldron needs to find solutions beyond armed war. Ideas of nonviolence joined with love and forgiveness can go a long way to establishing peace. While seemingly naïve, it has propelled change in America and South Africa.

Throughout his book, Tutu described the ravages of the apartheid ideology and implementation. The Afrikaner government established the hateful system in the 1940s. They passed laws that totally separated the races. Blacks, a majority of the population, were driven from their land. They were placed in schools not for enlightenment or the freedom of knowledge but to become subservient to white people. The apartheid system remained intact until it was dismantled in the 1990s.

In the decades before apartheid ended, Tutu used his religious post to critique the state-sponsored atrocity. He gave a voice to the voiceless. Moreover, he supported an economic boycott against South Africa.

Tutu described in his book how apartheid protesters often wondered whether apartheid would ever be overturned during this era. They were full of despair even though their cause was right and just. The final dissolution of the apartheid regime confirmed to them that their fight against injustice was commendable. With the end of the regime, Nelson Mandela then extended peace and forgiveness to his white tormentors instead of revenge and hostility. The revolution was astounding, and it revealed God's love at work.

After apartheid, Tutu's journey of love and peace continued when he led the Truth and Reconciliation Commission. This body allowed all apartheid victims to air the traumatic circumstances of their subjugation. The white perpetrators of apartheid also gave testimony in exchange for amnesty. This led to the route of forgiveness and healing on both sides. Tutu describes how the commission was a great success, and he fittingly titled a book about the commission *No Future without Forgiveness*.

In *Made for Goodness*, Tutu talks about the freeing effect of the African concept of ubuntu, which says that one's being and vulnerability is always joined to another's being and vulnerability. Seeing meaning via relationships with others can create human congruence.

Tutu's hope for the world rests on his unshakeable faith in God. Humankind, Tutu said, is made in God's image, and that image is fueled by empathy, justice, respect for humans, and forgiveness.

Humans can reflect unconditional love because that is how God views us. Tutu's life and writings are a testament to God's eternal love for us. He teaches us that we can overcome suffering when we love God and one another.

The Splendor of African American Women's Religion

The role of religion among many African American women has been a foundation of hope for freedom and self-worth. Alongside the US Constitution and related laws, the faith of black women has made our country a more tolerant place. African American women have endured unfathomable suffering through the centuries, yet divinity has saved them from despair and subjugation.

Black slave women endured horrific exploitation in the antebellum South. In her book *Labor of Love, Labor of Sorrow*, historian Jacqueline Jones delineates how whites violently oppressed black female slaves. They were forced to perform egregiously grueling work, and they suffered whippings.

In her book *Sisters and Saints*, religious historian Ann Braude described how slaveholders taught Christianity to their slaves even though Christianity could not be reconciled with slavery. Slaves were taught to be benign mothers and wives, yet they were separated from their families for profit.

Still, the essence of Christianity consoled many black female slaves. According to Braude, "While slaves had no legal rights, they knew that at the final judgment a signal standard would apply to all." The concept of a heavenly equality and freedom soothed them.

While the Civil War's Emancipation Proclamation and the Reconstruction Amendments assured freedom and rights, black women's conditions were mixed, Jones described. They experienced a greater family stability, yet they were also mired in "de jure segregation, disenfranchisement, white-initiated race riots, and lynching," she said. Moreover, they became sharecroppers and encountered the immobilizing force of debt peonage. "They did not own their equipment, nor could they market their crop independent of the landlord," Jones wrote.

Yet again religion offered solace. Black religious institutions grew and offered a soulful respite from the burdensome work of sharecropping, Jones wrote.

"Black women found a 'psychological center' in religious belief, and the church provided strength for those overcome by the day-to-day to business of living," she said. Additionally, black women became good leaders of the Methodist and Baptist churches.

From the 1940s to the 1960s, the modern civil rights movements began and flourished. Post-World War II, the NAACP saw its number of members increase and its antidiscrimination mission spread. The National Urban League challenged racism in America and fascism in the world. These epochal strides led to the dismantling of Jim Crow and disenfranchisement via "lunch-counter sit-ins, freedom rides and challenges to voting restrictions," Jones wrote.

In the 1960s civil rights movement, the black church was the conduit for civil disobedience. The beloved community ideal buttressed the church's efforts, and women in these institutions embraced the religiously inspired philosophy of nonviolence. While black men mostly led congregations, black women sang freedom songs in church, Jones said.

Furthermore, the Southern Nonviolent Coordinating Committee, suffused with religious iconography, treated black women protesters mostly as equals.

From the late 1960s to the present era, many black women have dealt with issues of employment, family, poverty, and community. As in the past, black women have relied on kin for spiritual and material dignity and subsistence. They have developed African American liberation theology that declares Jesus will liberate the oppressed.

America is a country of idealism and hope. It is a country in which principles of equality, freedom, self-esteem, and fairness are woven into our laws and praised in our religions. African American women's pining for a good God should be studied and lauded. Their religious roles show how faith can give balm to the oppressed and change the world for the better.

University of Michigan Professor Opines on Ferguson

The August 9, 2014, shooting and killing of unarmed African American teenage Michael Brown by white police officer Darren Wilson in Ferguson, Missouri, riveted and angered America, and the subsequent grand jury decision not to indict Officer Brown only accentuated the frustration and despair.

University of Michigan assistant professor in communications Josh Pasek has studied the conflagration since it first occurred and offers potential solutions for the existence of police violence in African American communities. While he wouldn't comment on the legal vicissitudes of the case as he is schooled in social science not the law, he suggests ideas that can offer guidance for people across the racial divide who care about the issue.

Pasek conducted a survey after the event about how African American and whites thought about the case. Approximately 90 percent of African Americans thought Wilson should be charged with murder while less than half of whites thought he should be charged.

"I think that divide speaks at its core to the real differences that black and white Americans have with the criminal justice system, their communities (and) the police," he said. "That is the underlying story for why there are a bunch of people (who are) upset."

Pasek says the often unfair reality of how police interact with African Americans stems from past racial discrimination, namely injustices like slavery and Jim Crow. He also suggests that what he calls implicit or cloaked racism most likely shaped the event and its aftermath.

Pasek says some white Americans might have latent derogatory views about other groups like African Americans. They have respect for diversity but may have hidden biases. They might be unaware of their prejudices, but they still exist.

"Those biases create disparities, and they create disparities on the level of how somebody like Officer Wilson would act, as well as how the Grand Jury might behave," he said.

Pasek further fleshes out his view on implicit racism while discussing racial profiling. He says the practice occurs because society asks police to determine whether a threat is real, and this decision about threat level is a subjective one.

Thus, in terms of the Brown case, it seems to me that Wilson might have felt the threat was real, yet the evidence showed his gratuitous antipathy. To be sure, Wilson testified to the grand jury that he felt precarious with Brown and that Brown was like a "demon." In the wake of the shooting, MSNBC's Chris Hayes interviewed Dorian Johnson, who had a different story. A friend of Brown's who witnessed the shooting, Johnson said Wilson used profanity and was antagonistic from the beginning of the altercation. Johnson's lawyer, Freeman Bosley Jr., said Wilson merely didn't value the life of a young African American man. This reality of targeting African American men seems likely in the Brown shooting.

Pasek has many views on how to heal the racial divide that has erupted since the killing of Michael Brown. Police need to represent the community they serve. The Ferguson police force is overwhelmingly white in a community where the vast majority of citizens are African Americans.

Deep transformation, Pasek said, happens externally and internally with the symbiosis of peaceful protests and building trust.

"There's no question that peaceful protests can spur change. The question is whether we as a country are willing enough to be introspective about the structural relations we build into the way communities are policed," he said.

Race relations have been the main paradox of America since the creation of our country. Pasek says the election of Barack Obama, our country's first African American president, ushered in the idea of a postracial America. Yet he says that idea is somewhat naïve, and our country has a long way to go to achieve true racial equality and justice. A substantive dialogue is urgently needed, he said.

If there is any benefit to the sorrowful Michael Brown case, it is that America is beginning to have this dialogue of awareness. Protests are swirling with defiance across the country, and Americans are holding signs that say Black Lives Matter and No Justice, No Peace. They are seemingly simple words, but they can change the racial landscape in America.

Toni Morrison and a Knowing So Deep

I have tremendous admiration for Toni Morrison. I have read many of her novels, and I am captivated by her immense intelligence and piercing empathy for African Americans and the human race. In the following pithy article, I humbly look at her vast mind's eye.

In her book of essays *What Moves at the Margin*, Morrison begins with a letter to black women called "A Knowing So Deep." In the missive, she lauds the earned achievements of African American women, whether it is via writing or other forms of expression.

"(Y)ou were like no other. Not because you suffered more or longer, but because of what you knew and did before, during and following that suffering," she said. "You had this ability to shape an untenable reality, mold it, sing it, reduce it to its transforming essence, which is knowledge so deep it's like a secret," Morrison writes.

The root of African American oppression stems from what she calls "slavery and silence," and black women have responded with authentic voices that affirm self-worth and jettison subjugation.

In subsequent essays, Morrison tackles race and the national conversation, yet what fascinates for humans most is the description of the process and message of her writing.

Morrison says the literary foundation for her work is slave narratives. She praises them for their courageous limning of singular yet universal slave experiences and their resulting call for redemption. They were often addressed to white abolitionists. Morrison suggests that their message to caring whites is "we are human beings worthy of God's grace" and that slavery must be abandoned.

Yet there are gaps in slave narratives that Morrison sees as her duty to fill. Because slave writers addressed their work to whites, they did not tell the more egregious parts of slavery. As a result, there is a lack of interior emotions in many slave narratives, Morrison said. It is her mission as a writer to cast off this veil shrouding black suffering. She employs her own memories as an African American woman and her imagination to reveal this pathos.

Morrison describes this process of creating good and beautiful novels: "It should have something to say in it that enlightens; something in it that opens the door and points the way. Something in it that suggests what the conflicts are, what the problems are. But it need not solve those problems because it is not a case study, it is not a recipe."

Thus, the content of her work is not didactic but evocative. She wrestles with ideas like the severely damaging effect of slavery on families and the inner lives of those who endured it; previously unknown heart-wrenching conflicts among men and women, sisters and brothers, mothers and fathers, and daughters and sons; notions of black and white beauty; and the numerous vicissitudes and complications of sexuality.

Her work gives balm and transcendence to her audience and helps humans know they are not alone in coming to terms with their history and its legacy. It frees and elevates all races with knowledge about the human condition.

At the end of her letter to black women, redolent of a lullaby, Morrison pays tribute to the souls of black women and their transformative value: "A disturbing disturbance that is not a hawk or a stormy weather, but a dark woman, of all things. My sister, my me—rustling, like life."

African American Economic Freedom and the Good American Soul

Americans should care about race in our country. From shootings at an African American church in South Carolina to the dispiriting comments by President Trump in Charlottesville in which he equated civil rights protestors with racist neo-Nazis, America has been saturated with discrimination and violence. Our country must fight for progress, both political and economic, in order to make America a more tolerant and just place. One way to achieve change is to look to the past in order to make a better future. The work of brilliant Columbia University professor is a good place to start.

Foner's book *Forever Free: The Story of Emancipation and Reconstruction* explores how former slaves and political leaders reacted to Civil War emancipation. For this essay, I will examine the dense yet vital economic issues to elucidate an important part of the America story on material hardship and dignity.

Foner unravels the story of the Civil War and America's struggle to provide civil equality and economic opportunity and justice to former slaves. He delineates how the most glorious example of freedom and equality achieved in American history occurred with the Civil War's

Emancipation Proclamation and the subsequent Reconstruction Amendments to the US Constitution that defined freedom.

President Abraham Lincoln freed slaves during the Civil War and oversaw the ratification of the Thirteenth Amendment, which abolished slavery during his lifetime. Later, Radical Republicans like Thaddeus Stevens and Charles Sumner helped pass the Fourteenth and Fifteenth Amendments, which called for equal protection under the law and the right to vote respectively. They also shepherded other civil rights legislation through Congress.

These political measures represented great advancement for America and former slaves, yet, as Foner asks, what did these achievements mean for economic freedom? In the debates over the Thirteenth Amendment, politicians talked about the importance of former slaves having capital benefits from their labor, yet how would this right take shape?

The crux of the debate centered on the dichotomy of the newly established idea of government intervention and the Northern notion of free labor. The former said government help and redistribution of land would provide economic freedom while the latter said that Americans of all races could advance themselves via individual hard work. As it often happens in America, the two sides were sometimes conflated and that can be a good thing.

This is a dialogue that predominated throughout the twentieth century and extends to today.

The history of the Civil War and Reconstruction animates this conversation about economics. It represents the great American truth that our country makes progress in fits and starts. Citizens face adversity but are forever trying to create a better union.

The system of slavery was one of unjust economic bondage. Slaves were property before the law. They had no legal rights. They were bought and sold and were often separated from their families. Racist and violent customs, like whipping, attempted to solidify whites' control over slaves.

Moreover, the economy profited from the institution in both the South and North. Southern planters amassed immense wealth from the slave system, and in the North, cotton was traded in New York and Europe. Factories made textiles out of the crop.

After emancipation, the Reconstruction era began. In terms of economics, the period is complicated yet thrillingly moving as it teases out what economic freedom means for Americans, both black and white. The dual ideas about government help versus self-reliance, in addition to their combination, speaks to the American idea of economic advancement.

For newly liberated slaves, ownership of land was paramount to their conception of freedom. Some slaves did not leave plantations and often divided land among themselves.

Moreover, they rejected the idea promulgated by whites that black freedom would be met with black indolence. Many former slaves' desire was to purchase land and work for themselves.

The actions of Union general William Sherman epitomized the dreams of newly free blacks. One of the first instances of economic justice after emancipation occurred in 1865, when he set aside land for newly liberated slaves on the South Carolina and Georgia coasts. He authorized blacks to have forty-acre plots and gave them mules that had been in the Union Army. Hence, he created the iconic phrase for blacks' economic dreams, Forty Acres and a Mule, and he initiated one of the first examples of land redistribution after the Civil War.

At the end of 1865, talk of more land redistribution like Sherman's spread throughout the South. Yet this idea was short-lived, and former slaves soon came to realize that the prospect of owning land was out of their reach.

At the same time, some white planters were regaining control of their governments and instated laws called Black Codes. In addition to circumscribing equal justice before the law and suffrage, these laws limited African Americans' ability to define their economic lives. Former slaves were required to sign labor contracts, and if they resisted, they would be arrested. African Americans could not leave one employer for another for better wages, thereby undermining a viable labor market.

While the hateful laws were mostly invalidated by the Freedman's Bureau, which offered aid and help to blacks in the transition to freedom, they underscored white Southerners' intransigence in transforming after emancipation.

Enter the Northern Republicans and the noble idea of free labor. As Northerners saw it, free market capitalism was the best way for Americans to prosper economically. Instead of the economic coercion of slavery, free labor would allow Americans to earn wages and later buy property in the form of a farm or a business. As Lincoln said, there was no such thing as a wage earner who was relegated to the same economic station for his entire life.

Yet because former slaves did not have land, a circumstance that if combined with free labor ideas could produce African American wealth, former slaves had to adapt to again working on plantations. No matter how hard they worked in agriculture in the form of sharecropping, the system did not allow African Americans to save enough money to buy property. The same was true in unskilled labor and domestic work.

Still, Republicans spurred economic progress for former slaves with their legislative efforts. In addition to the Civil War amendments, they passed bills that combined ideas of sharing resources with free labor concepts. Bills at the beginning of 1866 included a renewal of the Freedman's Bureau and the Civil Rights Bill. The former bill represented government aid while the latter embraced free labor values. Black Codes were abolished, and the right to make contracts, initiate lawsuits, and legally ensure the protection of person and property transpired.

Additionally, Republican governments in the South were supporting regional economic development. Instead of direct government action, they invested in economic industries like railroads. They hoped railroads would prompt the creation of factories and diversified agriculture that would replace the plantation system. They also gave tax incentives for Northern businessmen. Unfortunately, these efforts did not produce the desired effect. Moreover, there was corruption, a fact that opponents of Reconstruction used to castigate blacks for being unfit for leadership.

Disconcertingly, in the 1870s, the astonishing accomplishments of Republicans' Reconstruction ended. So-called Southern Redeemers revived the unjust practices of pre-Civil War society. Their previous attempts to oppress freed slaves in the form of Black Codes turned into total and lasting political and economic subjugation. Moreover, former slaves could not challenge the racist system lest they be lynched. The reason for the shift was economic. The country became mired in a recession, and the North no longer financed Southern Reconstruction governments. For former slaves, the collapse of Reconstruction meant de facto slavery.

The achievements of Reconstruction laid dormant for one hundred years until the 1960s civil rights movement. Leader Martin Luther King Jr. employed not only biblical references to buttress his cause but also the Reconstruction Amendments and legislation. In terms of economics, King was admirable, and he instituted economic initiatives like the Chicago Freedom Movement, which called for an improvement in black employment.

Reconstruction accomplishments will forever be set to be drawn on when movements of racial protest arises. In this instance of soul-searching for our country, citizens should open their hearts and build on the successes of past movements. Racial animus will transform into racial love and peace.

A Fighter for Love: John Lewis and an Urgent Map for the Future

Donald Trump's America is uncaring and coarse. To be sure, his treatment of immigrants and his insensitivity toward African Americans has damaged our country. As a nation, we need to come together and resist the exclusion of others. We need to realize we are all interconnected and are one human family. One way to bring us together is to look at American heroes who have risked their lives to make America a more humane place.

Civil rights leader John Lewis is one of those heroes.

John Lewis promulgates the idea that what affects one person affects us all. This concept is beautifully illustrated in Lewis's book *Across That Bridge*. Part memoir and part excavation of the meaningful ideas that fueled the civil rights movement, the book is dedicated to any human who wants to transform our country.

Lewis grew up in a farm near Troy, Alabama, as the son of a sharecropper. He was always a loving person as a result of a good family. His family was steeped in religion, and he had a solid belief in his innate self-worth.

While Lewis knew his own value, he nonetheless dealt with racist vitriol. His first encounter with racial injustice as a child occurred when he and his father went to the town of Troy. Making the trip to sell his crops, his father was demeaned by whites. Moreover, Lewis saw Jim Crow signs across the town. Later, he read about the *Brown v. Board of Education* Supreme Court decision. He was inspired by the possibility of integrated schools, yet his hopes faded as segregated schools remained.

Despite all these disparaging signs, Lewis later embarked on the voyage of his life, the civil rights movement, when he encountered Martin Luther King Jr. When the Montgomery bus boycott happened, Lewis was a teenager. He read about, then heard King talk about, a Christian response to the injustice of segregation and disenfranchisement. Lewis identified with King, feeling he was answering his prayers about how to confront the trap of segregation. King discovered a way to "see the power of love made manifest more than anything, to see hate eradicated and wrong made right."

Moved by King, Lewis eventually led the Southern Nonviolent Coordinating Committee in which scores of civil rights workers nonviolently traversed the South against Jim Crow and for voting rights.

Love and the idea of an inclusive beloved community undergirded the brave and innocent protesters. They met unthinkable violence with nonviolence. They revealed to the country that equality and suffrage are rights and to deny them is a crime against the human spirit. Lewis himself was beaten and jailed over forty times. Yet his and other civil rights workers efforts transformed the nation with passage of the Civil Rights Act and the Voting Rights Act, which ended Jim Crow and voter disenfranchisement respectively.

Love for Lewis and his fellow protesters was a combination of divinity and the truth that humans are innately good. Lewis described how the civil rights movement was already favored before it happened as God orders the world with a primordial goodness and care for fellow humans.

When white supremacists beat and jailed innocent protestors, they were living dishonestly. The truth that humans are joined together and are made to love one another was suppressed and obscured. Thus, the violence against the protestors damages the perpetrators just as much the victims. By using nonviolent tactics, the truth of human unity emerges.

In the decades since the civil rights movement, Lewis has received apologies from some of his white tormenters. He generously forgave them. This also is an emblem of love.

In the introduction to Lewis's book, historian Douglas Brinkley relayed a moving anecdote. When asked whether he was a Republican or Democrat, Brinkley always says he is wherever Lewis stands.

In the present fear about what happens next for America, we should all heed Lewis's decency and generosity. Looking at his example, we should stand up to nativism and racism. We should advocate for measures that will help people, not divide them. Indeed, we can strengthen the social safety net and promote policies that give everyone access to economic independence. As education offers innovation and opportunity, we should raise teachers' salaries to help students grow. With efforts like these, we can make our country a kinder place. Let love and empathy endure.

An African American Aviator and the American Dream

For Chauncey Spencer, his wings and the American dream were inextricably joined.

As recounted in his autobiography, *Who Is Chauncey Spencer?*, Spencer was a lifelong aviator who fought for racial integration throughout his life. The idea of racial comity for black aviators and beyond was part of his adamant belief in the necessity of equality and dignity for all Americans.

Spencer grew up in Virginia. His father owned real estate and worked at the US Post Office, and his mother was a poet and teacher. While he endured segregation in schools and churches, his parents were immersed in the conversation about black culture and civil rights. To be sure, they often hosted black artists and leaders like Paul Robeson and Thurgood Marshall.

In a way that defined the arc of his life, Spencer stood up for himself when dealing with racism and unfairness. It was a trait that he learned from his mother, who questioned leaders and wrote letters to the editors of newspapers.

"(My) mother's dogged determination was an example to me when I later needed that same kind of persistence or be swallowed by racial injustice," he said.

One of his earliest encounters with racial antipathy and protest occurred when he was in New York visiting his sisters in college. On his journey, he went to a restaurant for food but was told to leave because he was black. He bravely protested and appealed to the restaurant workers, but they did not demur. He was eventually physically removed. He was surprised that Jim Crow was present in the north.

By coincidence, he also heard black leader Marcus Garvey speak in New York and was captivated by his message stressing black heroes and the need for black economic self-determination.

Spencer knew he wanted to be a pilot since his youth. He remembers seeing a plane in the sky over his Virginia home, and the next day he built a plane of his own. Later, after being rejected at several schools because of his race, he earned an aviation certification from the University of Chicago in 1936. Many discouraged him, saying it was not possible for a black man to be a pilot. Yet he persevered and followed his dreams.

After flying across America as a young man, Spencer applied to be a flying cadet at Tuskegee Institute, a renowned aviation site, but he was too old to be accepted. Then he served as an instrument repairman, a first for blacks, at Patterson Field in Fairfield, Ohio. When Franklin Roosevelt penned Executive Order 8802, which ruled out discrimination within all federal agencies and industries having government contracts, Spencer was called upon to enforce it. A fight for racial progress proceeded. Armed with a stern commitment favoring integration and a changing legal landscape promulgating increasing civil rights for blacks, Spencer made lasting change.

His first assignment was to observe undercover Tuskegee Institute. What he saw disturbed him. Blacks were housed in small rooms and fed primitive food while whites ate at tables with linen cloths and were served by black waitresses.

Additionally, Spencer endured discrimination himself. As soon as he arrived at Tuskegee, a white supervisor told him to clean part of the site. Spencer protested that he was an instrument repairman, yet the supervisor persisted. Eventually he was arrested, but this was soon rescinded.

After his duty at Tuskegee, Spencer made a report, and changes were implemented. He was thrilled.

"Hopefully, a new day was dawning in which all Americans would be treated as Americans citizens without regard to race," Spencer said. "There was a long road ahead, but it was a step in the right direction."

Spencer's next assignment was to implement Executive Order 8802 at Patterson Field. When Spencer began there were no black supervisors and blacks held menial jobs. Spencer was committed to making Patterson a place where blacks could achieve economic independence and a high-wage job. Yet whites opposed him, saying they would quit if reforms were implemented. They categorically opposed integration. Still, Spencer prevailed, and blacks achieved skilled jobs like being physicists and printers.

For his valiant efforts, he was given an award by the Air Force in 1948.

Soon after, however, Spencer was told he was suspended from the air force for being a security risk. Spencer attributed the specious charge to the investigative melee of the McCarthy era in addition to a climate of racial ignorance and bigotry. Yet, as with previous hurdles, he fought it. Fellow friends in the air force defended his character, and with his bravery and forbearance, he kept his family together and remained tenacious about his innocence. He was exonerated in 1954.

In the last chapter of his life, Spencer left the air force and became an educator in California and Michigan. During this time, his daughter asked him if he wondered whether he had made racial progress. He said he believed he had. He said racial battles are fought and won perpetually, but there is a linear and gradual change. "I have to try to make an impact," he said about his life's motivation. "I have to fight for what I believe in."

In conjuring the vast array of African American leaders, Spencer is an important hero. He spent his life working for African American human rights, and he should be remembered for his life-changing contributions to our forever transforming nation. His example should inspire activists today to never give up on making America more equal and fairer. Let freedom fly.

Part 2

Judaism

All Are Human: Reaching for Peace in the Israeli-Palestinian Conflict

Introduction

The Israeli-Palestinian conflict is seemingly intractable as it is replete with human struggle, trauma, and despair. Yet is also full of understanding, decency, and good intentions.

The roots of the modern impasse can be traced to the 1948 war between Jews and Palestinians. Known to Jews as the Israeli War of Independence and to Palestinians as the Nakba, or catastrophe, the altercation established competing narratives. The Jewish narrative purports that the 1948 war was a heroic and valiant struggle to stave off Arab armies who were bent on annihilating the Jews and their nascent state. The Palestinian narrative says that 800,000 of their people were forcefully expelled from their homes and land by an uncaring Jewish military.

Despite these different narratives, a central facet of the conflict is how both Jews worldwide and Palestinians have suffered enormously. Jews have endured loathsome oppression, including slavery in the biblical era, the Spanish Inquisition, Russian pogroms, discrimination in Europe, and the Holocaust, according to Wayne State University professor David Weinberg. Palestinians have not only endured the Nakba, but also the current occupation, in which they are ghettoized and treated as inferior.

Thus, upon close examination of the conflict, a meaningful solution becomes apparent: both sides need to recognize their common trauma in order to see each other as human. War destroys and devalues the essentially benign quality of human beings. An airing of trauma will reconcile the two sides and establish a foundation for a peaceful, nonviolent solution. The view that the sides are too polarized to find peace is superficial and ignores the reality that both sides have been victimized.

Recognizing common trauma in the Israeli-Palestinian conflict has been part of the peace dialogue. Writing in the *New York Times*, Carlo Strenger, a psychology professor at Tel Aviv University, recommends that each side practice what he calls "talking cure diplomacy." Both sides have suffered collective trauma and thus must air their agonizing memories and circumstances. Palestinians must mourn for the Nakba in which so many of their people were displaced. At the same time, Israelis must voice their fears of annihilation. While many say these fears are a mere camouflage to justify colonial ambitions, these Israeli feelings are very real. They see the wars of 1948, 1967, and 1973 as moments when they could have been wiped out. The Holocaust is the root of this fear, Strenger said. He goes on to say that diplomacy must consider these worrisome narratives in order to move into the future. When this excavation of anguish is accomplished, a two-state solution can be realized, he said.[1]

In the *Jerusalem Post*, Jewish writer Tallie Lipkin-Shahak explores how to reconcile the greatness of the Jewish state with the horror of the Nakba. She laments how the Palestinian catastrophe is her people's vindication, and she rues how the sense of compassion among her fellow people has dwindled. She explains how Jewish trauma has had a paradoxical effect of hardening Jews' hearts. She says Israelis must find ways to compromise to live together with Palestinians in a two-state solution.[2]

The following oral history of Jew Doron Levin and Palestinian Elaine Rumman delineates the conflict in a deeply human manner. Both have strong feelings about the condition of their people, yet they additionally care about coexistence and empathy. With hopeful voices like theirs, solutions can be achieved.

Doron Levin

Doron Levin has worked as a business journalist in Detroit for many years. A member of the Jewish faith and affiliated with the reform movement, his life journey is a window into the Jewish experience in both Israel and the United States

Levin was born in Israel in 1950 in a settlement called Moshav Habonim, which his immigrant and pioneering parents helped build. The settlement was an agricultural community similar to a kibbutz but not as socialistic. His engineer father, Basil, was South African and a soldier who fought for the British in North Africa during World War II. Levin's mother, Ruth, was from Cleveland, Ohio. The couple met and got married in Israel. The name of their community—Habonim— means the builders in Hebrew. It was the moniker of a Zionist youth group Levin's dad had belonged to when living in South Africa.

Both Levin's parents immigrated to Israel in order to help with the establishment of the Jewish state. Basil helped secure the Negev for Israel.

In 1952, they left Israel for South Africa due to heath issues and hardships cultivating the land at Moshav Habonim.

When Levin was young, he and his family moved to the United States and settled in Pittsburgh, Pennsylvania. His parents, Reform Jews, sent Levin to Hebrew school and instilled Jewish values within him.

"We were proud Jews, affiliated with a house of worship," Levin recalled. "(We) celebrated the holidays at home, (and) I learned and knew about the scriptural connection between the Jewish people and the land of Israel."

As an adolescent, his parents encouraged him to read, and he vociferously poured through many books.

He read *Then Rise and Fall of the Third Reich* about Hitler, which horrified him, and he read Leon Uris's novel *Exodus*, which inspired him. The latter book typifies the narrative of the early Jewish state, namely the manner in which Jews were expelled from Europe, given Palestine by the British, and gloriously defeated villainous Arabs to establish a homeland for the Jewish people.

Later in life, Levin learned that Uris's novel was partisan, a story told from a strictly Jewish point of view. As a child, he didn't understand that there might have been a counternarrative, a version that told the Palestinian side.

"It's a complicated and difficult tale. There are injustices on both sides," he explained. "Part of the greatness of Israel is that Israel is full of people who understand this now."

While Levin read about the horrible discrimination Jews have suffered through the ages, he didn't encounter any significant discrimination in the United States. To be sure, he sometimes felt isolated as a Jew in a largely Christian society, and he did experience mild anti-Semitic discrimination, but America allowed him to have a good and productive life. Indeed, he raised a great family and has a successful career as a journalist.

Levin's decision to become a journalist had its roots in his childhood. Coming from an international background, he was always interested in current events, and he read the *New York Times* every day as a kid. His first foray into journalism began when he was intern at the *Sarasota Herald Tribune*. The journalistic atmosphere enchanted him.

Throughout his life, Levin has made many trips to Israel, all of which helped shape him as a Zionist. The first occurred in the summer of 1960. He visited his father's brother and met his family.

"I was very precocious. I was on my own. I got to know my cousins. And then I went to this settlement where I was born and got to know all these people who I never knew," he said.

While growing up the only thing Levin learned about Palestinians was that they were antagonistic to Jews. His early trip to Jerusalem only confirmed these feelings. When he visited Jerusalem, he read the *Jerusalem Post*, where he learned about snipers from the Palestinian side of the city.

Levin's most important trip to Israel occurred when he was a young adult after graduating from Cornell University. He went to the country thinking he wanted to write about it. When he landed in Israel, he was drafted into the army by virtue of his citizenship. For the first twenty-four months, he was in the field as a soldier, and then he served as a press person for the army. During this trip, he met his wife, Adina, a daughter of the Holocaust who was also in the army, which deepened his commitment to Zionism.

"I felt that going into the Israeli army would integrate me into that society. It would give me legitimacy and authenticity so that my opinion would count," he recalled. "I really felt passionate about the Zionist enterprise."

While Levin was in the army, he encountered a belief among his fellow soldiers that a single military defeat would bring about Israel's likely extermination. This notion of an existential threat stemmed from the wretched discrimination Jews have experienced, including the Holocaust. Seeing this feeling buttressed Levin's belief in the importance of a Jewish state.

One of Levin's most intriguing experiences in the field was when his unit was ordered to expel Jewish settlers from an illegal outpost in the West Bank. Afterward there was a fistfight in the barracks among soldiers arguing whether the government was justified in throwing Jewish settlers out of the West Bank territory. Levin said the experience foreshadowed the split in Israeli society and was the first time he encountered Israelis who favored staying in the West Bank.

After Levin returned from Israel, he went to Columbia Journalism School and began his job as a business writer. He came to Detroit as an adult where he has worked for the *New York Times*, the *Detroit Free Press*, and Bloomberg News. He is currently a radio host on SiriusXM, a contributor to Forbes, and an author specializing in the coverage of mobility and the global automotive industry.

Levin is pleased with Israel's maturity as a nation and that Israelis feel more self-confident than during the early years of their history. While the country still faces some threats from the Arab world, he relishes the fact that the country has established itself as a thriving state. It is this surety that has allowed Israelis, and Levin, to look back at the country's past and examine where they have gone wrong during their history. Levin's introspection allowed him to see the one-sided story of Exodus. He has also read Benny Morris, an Israeli historian who has questioned the Jewish narrative.

"He's trying to point out why the Arabs are right and the Israelis are wrong and why the Israelis are right and the Arabs are wrong," he said.

"I'm spending time reading because it's part of the journey I want to take."

Levin has many opinions about the peace process. He laments the fact that Palestinians didn't accept the UN partition plan in 1947. Favoring the two-state solution, he thinks Palestinians should recognize Israel's legitimacy and make compromises so they can have their own state. He is confident that peace can transpire. He believes Israelis are broadminded enough and decent enough and fair enough to create a society where everybody could coexist.

Elaine Rumman

Elaine Rumman is an eighty-year-old Palestinian American woman who suffered through the 1948 war and 1967 occupation in Israel. Despite endless war in the region, she maintained the sanctity of her family. Her husband, Jiries, worked for the Palestinian Liberation Organization and was passionate about his country and helping his people find justice.

Rumman had six children while living in Palestine, and she protected them all. Her husband moved to Ann Arbor after the 1967 occupation of the whole Palestine, and her family joined him in 1969. In Ann Arbor, she earned a social work degree from the University of Michigan even as she continued to take care of her family. After her husband died in 2001, she took up his cause and has spoken about the plight of Palestinians and possible routes for peace.

Rumman was born in 1930 in Palestine in a small town near Bethlehem called Beit Jala. Her life as a teenager was abundant and content. Her father, George, owned a general store, and her mother, Hanneh, was a generous homemaker.

The beautiful house where she lived had a yard that was full of fruit like figs and apricots in addition to a garden with vegetables. With her siblings, she used to build play houses from rocks near her house.

She said her mom, a Greek Orthodox Christian, instilled a deep faith and good values within her. Rumman educated herself by taking a psychology course and reading family magazines.

Rumman married her Palestinian husband, Jiries, in 1947 when she was about to turn seventeen. Educated and resourceful, he graduated from Bishop Gobat School in Jerusalem in 1932.

Rumman and Jiries were very cheerful during the start of their marriage, but then the 1948 war came, and their lives changed dramatically.

Rumman heard that war was imminent. On April 9, 1948, about a month before the Israeli War for Independence and the Nakba, she and her family learned from the news about the Deir Yassin massacre in which many people were expelled or killed. While her family was not displaced in 1948, the events worried Rumman's family.

In July 1948, Rumman had her first daughter, Maha, in the midst of the 1948 war. In 1949, Jiries rented a place to make a modern store that he and Rumman had dreamed of creating. They wanted to sell food and every kind of amenity. However, when they heard about fighting, they left the store with everything in it.

Later on, in 1949, her husband was captured by Jordanian soldiers. The Jordanians had wanted to annex the West Bank for themselves. Her husband was taken because he wanted to liberate Palestine and return to his land. Rumman was deeply frightened, yet Jiries was eventually released. However, because Jiries was a Palestinian political activist, they became political refugees and had to move to Gaza with the Egyptians. She was then pregnant again with her daughter Muna.

"My faith helped me handle things," Rumman recalled. "[Being a] political refugee means that you have to leave your home, family, warmth, and stability."

In 1955, Rumman and her family returned to Beit Jala because Jiries's father was sick. Rumman had had five children in six years and her last child after nine years. Jiries was hired as a supervisor in the West Bank of Jordan. Working for the Community Development Programme, he helped villagers with loans to build schools, roads, and health clinics.

Because Jiries was an activist and had a good reputation, the PLO hired him in 1964. Jiries was totally committed to the Palestinian cause. He made two trips to Central America to help his people. In the first trip in 1964, he was a PLO delegate to many countries in Central America, like Venezuela, Panama, and Cuba. He wanted to convince the heads of state to vote against Israelis in the UN, and if they couldn't, he asked them to abstain.

Later, he went to Honduras in March 1967, where he tried raising money for the PLO. When the war started in June, the PLO was disbanded, and he lost his job. He moved to Ann Arbor where he had a brother who was an engineering professor. He helped the family.

Meanwhile, Rumman was in Beit Jala during the 1967 war. Israelis bombed many houses in the town. She collected her children and women and children from other families and hid in the basement of her house. The memory of Deir Yassin came to her, and she fretted that the Israelis would take her beautiful daughters.

"That's the scary part for me," she said.

Still, Rumman and the other families in her basement ended up being safe.

After moving to Ann Arbor in 1969, Rumman decided she wanted to become a social worker. Her husband tried to dissuade her as he wanted her to take of their family, but she went anyway. She was on the honor roll at Washtenaw Community College and then went to University of Michigan, where she graduated in 1981. By studying vigorously at night, she managed to still help her family in their home. She cultivated an environment that was as normal as before she went to school.

Rumman then worked for both the Dearborn and Ann Arbor public schools.

Since her husband died, Rumman has given talks about Palestinians on the television station Community Television Network. She describes her experience during the wars as "traumatic and tough" and has strong beliefs about Palestinians being able to return to the land they lost during the Nakba and later wars.

"We have to go to the core of the problem: [Israelis] are living on Palestinian land. They occupy them, they kill them, they destroy their houses. They control every aspect of their life," she said.

She says she has a deep empathy for victims of the Holocaust but argues that her people were not involved. She thinks the one-state solution is the best remedy for her land.

And she says mutual love is possible for both groups.

"I am a person. I don't allow hate to come to my heart. I really forgive anybody. I can't hate anybody because hate makes you a prisoner of anger," she said. "I believe in one state and equal rights for all."

Conclusion

I believe in a two-state solution as I think the preservation of Israel is paramount for Jewish survival. Yet contemplating stances like a one-state solution and returning land lost in the Nakba are imperative as they reveal the desperate suffering of Palestinians. Still, gazing ahead is important as one cannot change the past but can change the future.

There are many groups working for empathetic change in the Israeli-Palestinian conflict. They see both Palestinians and Israelis as humans struggling for land and self-esteem. The Christian freedom group Sabeel and J Street are among the most effective.

Sabeel advocates for Palestinian liberation by underscoring cases of Palestinian oppression and employing Christian values. The group's leader, Naim Ateek, joined other clergy in writing the 2009 religious document Kairos, which describes Palestinian suffering and calls for change. It does not seek the end of Israel as a Jewish state but an end to the occupation.

Kairos says that we are all equal under God's eyes. This connotes how change can happen by seeing one another's common suffering and common morality. By treating one another with affection and hope, a dialogue can begin.

Additionally, Kairos addresses Jews directly about coexisting in the Holy Land: "Even though we have fought one another in the recent past and still struggle today," the website says, "we are able to love and live together."

J Street is a pro-peace, pro-Israel group that advocates for a two-state solution. It opines on the gamut of issues surrounding the conflict, like borders, settlements, security, and Gaza.

Part of J Street's mission is to see Israelis and Palestinians as equals.

To be sure, the group rues how for too long the pro-Israel dialogue has been defined by an us versus them mentality in which only one side can be a winner.

"(B)eing pro-Israel doesn't require an 'anti,'" the J Street website says. "Israel's long-term security actually depends on fulfilling the aspirations of the Palestinian people."

Like Sabeel, J Street calls Israeli and Palestinians to deal with one another with dignity.

Given all this action, one should be encouraged that a two-state solution might someday be achieved. By acknowledging the suffering of both sides, the Israelis and Palestinians should move forward and live side by side in peace and mutual care for one another.

The Resplendent Story of a Detroit Female Rabbi

Rabbi Michele Faudem, the longest serving female rabbi in Metro Detroit, is a shimmering emblem of the advancements women have made in America.

As a group, American women have made stirring strides since the advent of the women's movement in the early twentieth century. Women have garnered the right to vote. They have entered and thrived in once male-dominated professions. They have brought to the fore issues like domestic violence, equal pay for equal work, mental illness, and health care. Faudem's accomplishments are a legacy of women who have strived before her.

Faudem is a conservative Jewish rabbi who grew up in West Bloomfield, Michigan. She traveled and lived in Israel with her family during her high school years. She participated in Israel's National Service program for two years.

She always knew she wanted to be a rabbi, a vocation suffused with goodness and erudition.

"I liked studying. I liked how it made me feel part of a group with a big purpose. I liked all the rituals, and the deep meaning attached to them," she said of her decision.

The drive for the ordination of women rabbis, buttressed by the women's movement at large, was cumbersome and took place piecemeal from the 1970s to the 1980s. However, by the time Faudem came of age in the 1990s, becoming a female rabbi was not unusual and was generally accepted.

"I never knew I couldn't be a rabbi. I had no clue I couldn't be one," she said.

To be sure, her parents encouraged her to be anything she wanted, and they never saw her gender as an impediment. Moreover, there was no gender bias in her education.

Faudem said it is no coincidence that secular feminists like Gloria Steinem and Betty Friedan were Jewish. The Jewish condition of being an outsider most likely informed their activism, Faudem said.

"It's the whole story of freedom, of striving for more (in order to) make people's lives better," she said.

As a rabbi, Faudem contributes to the beautiful Jewish tradition of education. She teaches the Melton Program, a curriculum developed by the Hebrew University in Jerusalem. The two-year program instructs Jews and non-Jews alike about the Jewish religion, culture, heritage, and history, according to the Jewish Federation of Metropolitan Detroit website.

Faudem likes the portability of Judaism and the organic nature of Jewish texts like the Torah.

"It means something different ever year. I'm someone different. I read it based on where I am, what I'm dealing with (and) what I've seen in the past year," she said.

Like most female rabbis, Faudem struggles with the tension between the tradition of the Torah and other texts with the current reality of feminism and modernity. She says that while the Torah can be interpreted from a feminist viewpoint, it must also be understood that the text was written in a certain patriarchal context.

Women have to have confidence and self-esteem to understand they can be rabbis, Faudem said. They should know they have a lot to articulate. With her devotion to the Torah and her loyalty and love toward Israel, she reveals how female rabbis can have a place at the rabbinic table.

Viktor Frankl and the Enduring Ideas of Love and Hope

Viktor Frankl's witness is heroic. A former prisoner in the Nazi concentration camps of Auschwitz and Dachau, he wrote a moving book entitled *Man's Search for Meaning*. The book delineates his distressing experience of Nazi evil and the subsequent wonder of finding love and hope out of the physical and psychic atrocity.

Frankl limns a picture of German concentration camps that is unimaginably disturbing. He explores the shattering emotions Jews felt during the Holocaust. First came shock and then numbing apathy.

When he and others went to Auschwitz, they had no notion of how ravaging their plight would be. Frankl said they endured a psychiatric state called delusion of reprieve, which meant that they hoped everything would be all right. They entered the Auschwitz station and were greeted by prisoners who had uniforms and shaved heads. They seemed calm and fed in a good manner, yet little did Frankl and others know that this group of prisoners was hiding the evil that would ensue.

Frankl and 1,500 others resided in a shed made for a couple hundred. They were soon to be separated for work or the gas chamber. Frankl would live, but the majority would die. Frankl was a psychiatrist, and a manuscript of his life's work was stolen from him. He said the taken manuscript was like losing a mental child.

Later, the Jews were told to remove their clothes for a shower, and they were eventually shaved and then whipped by Nazis. Many prisoners had thoughts of suicide.

"We really had nothing now except out bare bodies," Frankl said. "All we possessed literally was our naked existence."

Then came apathy. Feelings were dulled about being surrounded by the dead and the dying. Prisoners were famished. Beatings were commonplace, and bread was rationed. Frostbite existed while prisoners performed onerous work. Lack of concern for life was a mechanism for self-preservation and defense.

Yet out of these wretched conditions came meaning. Frankl realized love for others could not be extinguished.

"For the first time in my life I saw the truth as it is set into song by so many poets, proclaimed as the final wisdom by so many thinkers. The truth—that love is the ultimate and the highest goal to which man can aspire," he said.

With love as a foundation, hope springs. To be sure, Frankl cites many examples of how even in the midst of unfathomable evil, the human spirit can survive and flourish.

Love and hope transpire when humans feel they have a future. In one example, a suicidal prisoner thought about his child. It was a mental escape that kept the war in abeyance and allowed him to see the beauty of parenting. Another suicidal prisoner, a scientist, thought about an unfinished text and how he would work on it. He was buoyed by those thoughts of the future.

Frankl's Holocaust experience and the meaning he wrested from it segued into a theory of psychiatry he invented called logotherapy. Logos means meaning in Greek, and Frankl says a deep hunger for meaning is the central motivation for humans. He cited a poll in which 89 percent of people surveyed said they needed something in order to live, and 61 percent said there was someone or something for which they would die.

The crux of his therapeutic idea is to present a range of meanings to his patients so that they might find what is most meaningful to them. He says true meaning is not found in the psyche but in the world. He argues that humans find purpose by giving themselves to another person or to a cause.

Frankl says he is optimistic even in the midst of hardship. He cites how even in the evil nadir of the Holocaust, some were heroic by soothing others and sharing food. He says heroes and saints are in the minority, but he is convinced that every human can strive for goodness. Even with greed and hurt, humans can pray that humanity might change. When a universal brotherhood is achieved, meaningful love and peace will occur.

A Good Look at Judaism and the Dignity of Nonviolence

Nonviolence is a gallant practice and way of life. All religions have elements of the idea, and applied to the world's war zones, the principle will transform humans and nations in a just and decent manner.

The Israeli-Palestinian conflict is one area where nonviolence is desperately needed, and the Jewish faith has the potential to change the seemingly intractable dispute. Jews and Arabs throughout the world care about the issue. To be sure, the conflict can be seen as a microcosm of global strife, and its resolution might lead to a diminishment of violence across the Middle East.

In the book *Subverting Hatred*, Conservative Jewish rabbi Jeremy Milgrom writes an essay for an anthology in which he describes his despair over the Israeli-Palestinian conflict. He feels sorrow about the usurpation of Palestinian land. While some Israelis say ceding land might spell the end of Israel as a Jewish state, Milgrom says the opposite is true: the ever-escalating war and violence in the country is unsustainable.

In his essay, Milgrom examines Jewish scripture with the hope of opening a dialogue about nonviolence. He concedes that a lot of Jewish scripture exhibits violence, yet he shows that nonviolent ideas and stories also predominate. Based on love and integrity, the latter should prevail, he said, and the world can be renewed in the image of a benign God.

As a preface to his discussion of nonviolent Jewish texts, Milgrom quotes thinker Steven Schwarzschild to elucidate his conception of peace or shalom. To paraphrase, Schwarzschild says peace is not merely the absence of war but a sense of good human traits like wholeness, honesty, grace, and justice. When these human powers work together, the world will know peace. When any of them is excised, conflict arises.

The Torah prods humans to love one another and sees this emotion of affection as an instrument to stem hatred and violence.

Thus, a quote from the Jewish scripture: "Thou shall not avenge nor bear any grudge ... but thou shalt love thy neighbor as thyself" (Leviticus 19:18 KJV).

Milgrom also shows how Jewish texts and rabbis have rejected militarism through the ages. One example is the denunciation of Bar Kochva, a Jew who instigated a revolt against Romans but was routed by them. According to Joseph Telushkin's book *Jewish Literacy*, after the battle, Jewish men were sold into slavery and women were forced into prostitution. Telushkin said it was the worst cases of Jewish suffering before the Holocaust.

When looking at these types of conflicts, everyone should see the futility of war and the importance of making peace. In the Middle East, where the sides of discord are often blurred and chaotic, the need for nonviolent dialogue is acutely vital. We are all in this world together, and we must work for interfaith and international comity.

Milgrom has a brilliant idea about what it means to achieve nonviolence. Justice should come first, he said, and then peace will follow. An aggrieved human has the right to ask for justice. Peace without justice only "feeds the seeds of future oppression," Milgrom said.

At the end of his essay, Milgrom argues for the Jewish concept of takanat hashavim, which calls for misappropriated land to be restored. Palestinians should be given their own land in a manner that will not circumscribe the sanctity of Israel and the Zionist principle of self-determination. This all should be achieved nonviolently.

The study of religions, including Judaism, reveals how violence corrodes, and rather than solving conflicts, it exacerbates them. Nonviolent alternatives have a good chance of prevailing even as Israel and Palestine and much of the world are consumed with war. Nonviolence should take root as it is buttressed by love, which is infinitely more powerful than hate. Citizens of the world should be grateful for the good in the world, and more love might transpire.

Styron Finds Meaning for the World amid Auschwitz's Evil Nadir

William Styron was a truly decent man with immense literary gifts.

Author of scores of essays and novels, he mined the pathos of life and the soul-shattering consequences of humankind's impetus to dominate and subjugate others. His genius, intertwined with bold actions in his life, led to the creation of great literature. His limning of the human struggle, both physical and emotional, helps people transcend traumatic conflict and revive what it means to be human.

For this essay, I will focus primarily on his masterpiece *Sophie's Choice*.

Sophie's Choice is about the Holocaust, in which Germans slaughtered millions of people, including six million Jews. People in the book deal with the unendurable. The book reveals the Holocaust's evil nadir and how the Nazis perpetrators subjugated human victims. Despite the darkness of the novel, one is left with empathy for the book's characters.

Before examining the vicissitudes of the novel, we should look at the roots of Styron's brave witness.

A dramatic precursor to *Sophie's Choice* was *The Confessions of Nat Turner*, which dealt with a slave revolt and the unjust bondage that led to it before the Civil War.

Styron's creation of the book stemmed from his affinity for black people during his youth. Styron was a product of both his family and the community he grew up in Newport News, Virginia. His parents were respectable people who were both enlightened about race and indignant about the injustices that afflicted black people. Styron adhered to these views. Moreover, while Styron grew up with Jim Crow and segregated schools, he made contact with black people when he made visits to an all-black college named Hampton Institute to listen to an orchestra.

"It was surely these memorable evenings at Hampton that caused me far back in my childhood to begin a long process of identification with the Negro people and the Negro spirit," Styron said.

Styron's portrait of slavery in turn led to *Sophie's Choice*. By writing about the barbaric system of bondage, he became aware of other examples of radical suffering. One event was the Holocaust.

Styron began thinking about writing *Sophie's Choice* in the 1960s. During this decade, he began a friendship with writer Hannah Arendt, who had chronicled totalitarianism and Nazi evil in *The Origins of Totalitarianism* and *Eichmann in Jerusalem* respectively. Both shared feelings about the unjust domination of others. Given his valiant account on slavery, Arendt encouraged Styron to delve into the momentous task of writing about the Holocaust. She told him to be courageous and to use his artistic imagination to create a meaningful and authentic account.

Styron was further propelled to write about the Holocaust after visiting Auschwitz in the early 1970s. He saw Birkenau, the part of Auschwitz where millions of Jews were exterminated via death ovens. The wooden barracks were no longer there, yet other hideous brick buildings were where the "numberless damned" had existed.

Sophie's Choice tells the life of Sophie, a Pole who faced unimaginable hardship while at Auschwitz during World War II, and her association with Nathan, a Jew afflicted with mental illness. The narrator of the book is Stingo, an aspiring writer who befriended the couple and became a witness to their woeful life circumstances. The agonizing truth about them is gradually revealed to a shocked and disheartened Stingo.

Sophie builds a relationship with Stingo and tells him how her father was a noble man who tried to save Jews during the war. Yet he was actually a rabid anti-Semite, a fact Sophie was hiding in order to cloak the hardship of her lifetime, namely the Nazis ordering her to choose one of her children to be killed at Auschwitz.

Sophie's dealings with Nathan compounds the sorrow of the story. Nathan is a charming and intelligent Jew whose obsession with the Holocaust exacerbates Sophie's acute stress about the atrocity. Moreover, Nathan has a secret of his own, mental illness, which Stingo unearthed by talking with his brother. His mental malady made his relationship with Sophie upsetting and volatile. To be sure, it overwhelmed her.

Sophie's Choice leaves readers with a broken heart, yet the story makes people care about the messiness of the human heart when encountering sheer evil. Despite the dispiriting ending, the characters in the book exhibit bravery in trying to come to grips with the unfathomable. Stories like these need to be told to future generations so that something like the Holocaust will never happen again. By exposing one of the gloomiest corners the world has ever encountered, Styron paves a way for its opposite, namely love for humans in all their splendid diversity.

A Modern-Day Exodus: The Heroic Redemption of Ethiopian Jews

Asher Naim was appointed Israeli ambassador to Ethiopia in the 1990s, and his mission was to help Ethiopia's Jews, also known as Falashas, to go to Israel. His story is recounted in his wondrous book *Saving the Lost Tribe*. The feat became known as Operation Solomon.

From the outset, Naim made his intentions of bringing Falashas home to Israel clear to Ethiopia's leaders. His efforts would be hard. He had to work with President Mengistu Haile Miriam, also known as the black Stalin of Africa. His aide Kasa Kabede was an elite who had attended Hebrew University. While Naim had Israel in common with Kasa, Kasa was still a spokesman for Mengistu and his draconian leadership.

Naim's introduction to the Falasha people at the Israeli embassy was guided by Zimna Berhane, a Jewish activist who had made helping Falashas his life's work. The Falashas came to the embassy from the village of Gondar. They were tired and without homes and needed money and food. They wanted education. They owned livestock but couldn't own land. They were excluded from food rations because they did not live in Addis Ababa, the capital of the country. They were persecuted by Ethiopian Christians for allegedly spreading illness.

Despite these burdensome hardships, the Falashas maintained their religious faith. Naim met with a religious leader near Addis Ababa named Kes. He told Naim he wanted to go to Holy Land to be with his people, and Naim said that was his reason for being in Ethiopia. While the rabbinic law in the form of the Mishnah and the Talmud had never reached the Falashas, their faith had many similarities to Judaism at large. To be sure, Kes and his people believed in the God of Israel and the law from Sinai. They believed in Jewish holidays like Yom Kippur and Passover in addition to the coming of the Messiah, who would return exiles to the Holy Land.

The 1991 Operation Solomon was an astounding humanitarian rescue. Naim and his cohorts worked with George H. W. Bush to facilitate the operation. Bush, via General Brent Scowcroft, drafted a letter to Mengistu and Kesa urging cooperation. Despite previous intransigence, Kasa talked with Naim and Berhane about a monetary contribution in exchange for the Falasha exodus. They settled on several million dollars, which the American Jewish community raised in few days. On May 25, 14,000 Falashas boarded planes and went to Israel.

Naim's great rescue of the Falashas underscores the values of generosity and freedom that are so dear to the Jewish way of life. Moreover, the relief given to the Falashas reflected America's tradition of supporting human rights across the world. As Naim said of his successful campaign: "No matter what the price, no matter what the risk, it was imperative that every effort was made to redeem the life of another Jew." While the event occurred decades ago, it shows that human care will prevail over oppression.

Part 3

Christianity

Gospel Train: The True Meaning of Christmas

My mom always tried to make sure Christmas was abundant and full of love for my siblings and me. She would shop early and buy us beautiful things like clothes and jewelry, as well as irreplaceable gifts like a meaningful book or a piece of art work. One Christmas, when I had become interested in writing, she gave me an anthology of newspaper writing. I loved it.

My mom grew up poor. Her mother was an alcoholic, and she lived with her grandmother, who loved her, in Massachusetts. While she was tight-lipped about her youth, I knew her Christmases were probably sparse and full of angst, given the ache she must have felt about her absent mother. Still, her unshakeable spirit allowed her to thrive as an adult. I grew up hearing stories about how my mom prevailed over adversity. She dazzled with smarts and accomplishments.

So, in December 2013, when I heard that the Republicans had cut food aid to the poor and voted on a budget that would end unemployment benefits, I trembled with fear and anger thinking of my mom's struggle. The poor are not inferior or indolent. Some Republicans have resisted this attitude toward the deprived. Ohio Governor John Kasich said the GOP was mercilessly waging a war on the less fortunate.

Talking about the lapsing of unemployment benefits, President Obama said Americans would lose "a vital economic lifeline at Christmas" and that "we are a better country than that."

He's right. All of us are better than that.

In pondering the plight of the poor, I reread a book called *God of the Oppressed* by James H. Cone. The book delineates how poor African Americans have liberated themselves from the bondage of slavery, de facto slavery like sharecropping, Jim Crow, and disenfranchisement via God and Jesus Christ and African American protest culture.

While slavery and Jim Crow have been eradicated, African Americans still bear the brunt of poverty in America. Whites and Hispanics make up a substantial percentage of poverty, but African Americans endure a greater amount.

Cone describes how African American theology gives balm to the poor and discriminated. The belief systems include how the God of Moses and Jesus Christ have been life and spirit-saving forces for African Americans. The Exodus story, in which Jews were freed from Egyptian slavery, has been a spiritual bulwark for the struggle against white supremacy.

Moreover, Jesus's life and teachings in the Gospels have given African Americans moral sustenance. Jesus's good news of embracing the poor and afflicted resonated with them. The New Testament says: "Blessed are ye poor, for yours is the Kingdom of God. Blessed ye that hunger now, for ye shall be filled" (Luke 6:20–21 KJV). The symbols of the cross and resurrection were God's way to show solidarity with the poor and marginalized. Jesus died for them so that they would find relief and freedom.

Harriet Tubman protested the oppressive system of slavery by invoking both Moses and Jesus in her slave spirituals. She yearned for release from bondage and deliverance toward liberation based on the iconic biblical figures.

Modern African American artists and activists have been equally important for African American freedom and equality. The witness of Martin Luther King Jr., Zora Neale Hurston, Fannie Lou Hammer and Toni Morrison has nurtured African American vitality with courage and grace.

The urgent truth is that African Americans have and should continue to speak and write about both their oppression and triumph. When they convey the truth about their experience, we become more humane as a society.

My mom was not a slave, or a sharecropper, or injured by Jim Crow, but she did endure enormous hardships like poverty and loneliness that African Americans and humans of all races have encountered. Looking back at Christmas 2013, we should reject detestable lies about those who struggle because of race or economic privation. Instead, we should center our efforts on giving love and aid for the helpless.

As Cone said: "We do not struggle in despair or but hope, not from doubt but from faith, not out of hatred but out of love for ourselves and for humanity."

Merry Christmas, MoMo. I love you.

Pope Francis and a Democratic Mercy

Pope Francis is a moral role model, and his most important credo is the idea of mercy.

Pope Francis's tender empathy for humans mirrors Jesus's mercy. Jesus, one can divine from Francis, has an infinite care for sinners, the spiritually lonely and misunderstood, and the poor and the marginalized. Jesus loves everyone and includes everyone. His mercy is thus a mesmerizing form of radical egalitarianism, a humane and vast democracy that reaches every corner of the world.

Jesus's form of moral democracy has captivated Pope Francis since he started his tenure as leader of the Catholic Church. He has accepted gays and divorced couples. He has lived simply and frugally as a form of solidarity with the poor. He has a striking humility, having said that he is foremost a sinner and that he has moral doubts.

In his book *The Church of Mercy*, Pope Francis described the idea of mercy on an individual and societal level. Humans sin and sometimes feel distressed for a host of reasons like unfairness and moral exclusion. Yet Francis exhorts that God and Jesus never abandon humans. He says

God can satisfy spiritual hunger and the miracle of Jesus's example gives humans grace to overcome any ethical or spiritual barriers.

Pope Francis has deeply felt opinions about mercy on a global societal scale. One of his paramount aims is to help the poor as evidenced in Jesus's gospels of mercy. Francis argues for a church "that is poor and for the poor." In Francis's book, he says that poverty is a form of injustice that must be improved. He calls for everyone to engage in some kind of social justice. Humans must strive to be like the apostles who followed Jesus even when they endured persecution, he said.

In his discussion of the poor, he says reaching for a societal good does not mean succumbing to an oppressive regime, presumably, he means, like Communism.

Pope Francis added that in trying to be a servant like Jesus, humans must dismiss false idols like vanity, careerism, and dominating others. His ministry reveals that inequities can be confronted and ameliorated if believers in God jettison selfishness. Humans need to be humble in order to assist others.

Unitarian Parishioner Nurtures Love and Diversity

Jill Crane fights for tolerance and inclusion at her Unitarian Church in Grosse Pointe, Michigan.

As director of adult religious education, Crane reaches out to her fellow parishioners with a bevy of programs that feed the spirit and stretch the intellect. There are women's book clubs, writing groups, poetry study groups, and a nascent idea about starting a philosophy gathering.

"Everybody's invited to everything," Crane said. "It is not a closed anything."

The Unitarian Church was formed in the sixteenth century and believes in the importance of equality and freedom. Rooted in Judaism and Christianity, among other religions, the church creates a welcome and safe place for all humans.

Here are a few past Unitarians: Paul Revere penned the pamphlets that spurred the American Revolution, and Herman Melville portrayed the contradictions and pathos of America with his literature. Activist Margaret Fuller advocated for women's rights, and Ralph Waldo Emerson authored facets of American philosophy.

With her work for Grosse Pointe Unitarian Church, Crane's efforts are a microcosm of how these renowned members made a belief system full of love and empathy. She communicates hope for the transformative role of the church both locally and globally.

One foundation of the church is its support for a democratic structure. Members are encouraged to speak their minds and develop their own voices. The open community of members is expected to respect diverse viewpoints.

"We Unitarians are known for talking and discussing," Crane said.

To be sure, Crane said when her congregation comes together as a group, people have no fear standing up and disseminating their opinions.

Within this context of free speech, Crane's programs run seamlessly as members can explore both their individual spirituality and care for the world. Indeed, they can find their identities and cultivate the principle of social justice in order to diminish society's inequities.

To me, perhaps the most thrilling part of Crane's work is overseeing the adult forums, which include speakers from within and outside the church. They talk about the vulnerable and the marginalized in order to support important pillars of the Unitarian Church, namely love and acceptance.

One of the most salient forums was a speech by a couple of transgender individuals. The church had voted to be a LGBTQ-welcoming church, and Crane said she relished the decision. She said tolerance is paramount, and she voiced her support for the coming out of Bruce Jenner as a woman.

Another forum was a debate on affirmative action. Two individuals— one black, one white—argued about whether the concept achieved equality. Paradoxically, the black speaker opposed the practice while the white one advocated for it.

"Every person is valued. Black, white, gay, and straight," Crane said of the adult forums. "We are very interested in human rights and dignity."

Crane said she sees her church as an island of progressivism in a sea of more conservative Grosse Pointe values. Still, she thinks her church can have an impact on the Grosse Pointe community.

"We try to get the message out, but it's not easy," she said. "Everyone is welcome."

Feminist Theology and the Importance of Women

Women's lives matter and learning about Christian feminist theology can restore women's dignity in a church and tradition that sometimes discards them.

In her book *Feminism and Christianity: The Essential Guide*, author Lynn Japinga gives humans hope about women and faith. Japinga excavates the stories of courageous women in the history of the Christian church and additionally critiques biblical scripture and theology for its stories and ideas about women. In Japinga's account, women's voices are valued and their efforts praised.

Japinga can best be described as a moderate feminist. She believes in the reality of patriarchy, yet she stresses that men are part of the solution to curbing it. She says that men and women should work together in order to create a peaceful world in which both sexes can follow God's benign and equal intention for them.

Japinga catalogues the stories of female theologians and leaders in a stirring manner. The examples are numerous, yet the message is clear: women have made enormous contributions to Christian thought and practice through the ages.

Here is one Christian woman:

Anne Hutchinson was a skilled teacher and theologian in seventeenth-century Puritan America. She led Bible studies for women, and her sermons were so captivating that men began to listen too. Puritan elders were aghast at her influence. According to the National Women's History Museum, they castigated her not only because she was an opiniated woman but also because of her message that humans could receive salvation by a direct relationship with God. In contrast, Puritan leaders believed that good deeds were needed to achieve God's grace. Hutchison was put on trial for heresy and banished from Massachusetts. She settled in more liberal Rhode Island.

Japinga examines Jewish scripture and the New Testament and their interpretations by humans in order to jettison sexist views and accentuate favorable ones.

The garden of Eden story in Genesis is perhaps the most widely discussed tale about gender discrimination. The story is as follows: God said human beings could eat from any tree in the garden of Eden save for the tree of knowledge of good and evil. Eve was tricked by a serpent into eating fruit from the latter tree, and she gave some to Adam. Thus, sin existed.

As a result of this story, some men have accused all women of bringing sin to the world. Tertullian said every woman should be punished for Eve's sin and that women were like devils. Saint Augustine said women had immature minds.

Japinga describes the consequences of this dishonest idea about women being inferior in creation and causing human sin. Women were "defective, limited and not quite in the image of God." Moreover, they were "sexual temptresses." These ideas have made their way through history. Indeed, women today are sometimes valued not for their minds but for their sexuality, Japinga said.

Jesus was most likely a feminist despite the patriarchal views of Him that have predominated in the Christian tradition, Japinga said.

She described the patriarchal interpretation as follows:

Jesus only chose male disciples and mostly associated with male leaders. Jesus was kind to women, but he didn't see them as equals in the church. He didn't make any substantial efforts to challenge patriarchy. These ideas support traditional roles for women and the notion of female submissiveness, Japinga said.

Yet evidence from the Gospel offers a more nuanced perspective: Jesus's mother, Mary, was, among other women, present at the crucifixion. Mary Magdalene was a confidant to Jesus and a crucial part of the resurrection. Moreover, many stories show that Jesus valued women. He encountered a Samaritan woman and asked her for a drink even though such contact was forbidden. She discovered He was the Messiah and told others about Him and others believed her. He was following a real and good God who saw the truth that women are worthy of respect.

Japinga's thoughtful analysis allows women to be both feminists and Christians. The Bible is a book about life and liberation. Patriarchy exists in the Bible, yet it overwhelmingly supports reaching for equality, justice, change, and love. Japinga invites both men and women to solve issues related to gender and empathy and thus know the loving and true essence of God.

Unraveling PTSD: The Challenges of Chaldean Refugees in Detroit

The American story of Chaldeans, Catholics from Iraq, is one of trauma and healing. They are a brave and resilient people who have fled their ancestral home in the Middle East for a better life in America.

Some four hundred Chaldeans are arriving in Detroit, Michigan, every month, and they are leaving Iraq due to religious persecution for being Christian. As a result of killings, torture, combat violence, and trepidation generated by war, one of Chaldeans' major obstacles is dealing with PTSD. They have endured unfathomable suffering in war-torn Iraq and have psychic scars that drain and debilitate.

Enter Martin Manna. Manna, president of Detroit's Chaldean Community Foundation, has built an incredible human service organization that helps Chaldean refugees adapt to life in America, which often means trying to heal PTSD. To be sure, Manna said approximately 40 percent of refugees have the malady when coming to America.

"It's a lot of pressure," Manna said. "They have been through one mess after another. There's a lot of nervousness and fear."

The context in which Chaldeans are fleeing due to ISIS is crucial to understanding their trauma, Manna said. Over two hundred thousand Chaldeans have been displaced from northern Iraq merely because they are Christian. ISIS fighters painted the letter N on Christian homes for the word Nazarenes, which denotes a belief in Christianity. ISIS told Christians that they had twenty-four hours to convert to Islam, leave, or die.

Manna said members of ancient Christian communities are dying because they love Jesus Christ.

Before coming to America, Chaldean refugees, many from the intellectual class, have often languished in refugee camps in other Middle East countries. Manna said when Chaldeans come to America, they have appreciation for our way of life. Though they receive limited government assistance, Chaldeans are pleased to be in our country.

"They're very thankful for the peace they're getting here, (and) the fact that they have religious and economic freedoms," Manna said.

The vicissitudes of PTSD are intricate and varied, and the journey to wholeness is not linear or the same for everyone.

"Each individual case is different. You just don't know how many layers there's going to be and what the root of the problem is," Manna said.

Manna said the mental health services are combined with a spectrum of other social services that helped Chaldeans make Detroit their home. The hope is that the immigrants will join the already booming Chaldean community in which 61 percent own businesses like food markets.

"We try to put the new Americans on a pathway to prosperity (and) a pathway to independence," he said.

Manna rued that Iraqi Christians might be both forever expunged from Iraq and be refugees without homes. He believed the Bush administration was incorrect in invading the country in 2003, yet he loves America. To be sure, he said one of the greatest things about our country is its acceptance of immigrant minorities of every ethnicity and religion.

Manna's example shows the world why freedom matters, and his people represent the best of America.

How Mary Magdalene Gave Birth to Christianity

Mary Magdalene is a woman worthy of study and veneration.

In Bruce Chilton's book *Mary Magdalene: A Biography*, the author presents Mary in a thought-provoking way.

Mary met Jesus in her twenties. Compelling and complex, Mary was instrumental in shaping vital tenets of Christianity. As Jesus's most treasured disciple, she witnessed the resurrection and then disseminated its meaning. In His risen state, writer Bill Bright said, Jesus proved that He was the Son of God and could thus be a savoir for all humans. This reality meant that Jesus could not only promise eternal life but also give followers exoneration from unjust bondage and forgiveness for sins. Mary understood this.

The road to Mary's sighting of the resurrection began when she anointed Jesus weeks before His death in Jerusalem. Anointing was widely accepted in the ancient world for things like healing and attending the dead after burial. For Mary, her anointing portended Jesus's death and the suffering He would endure.

Days after Jesus's crucifixion, Mary, along with other followers of Jesus, Mary of James and Mary of Salome, went to Jesus's tomb for anointing and found it open. There they had a startling vision of an angelic young man clothed in white. "Be not affrighted: Ye seek Jesus of Nazareth, which was crucified. He is risen; he is not here," the young man said. "But go your way, tell his disciples" (Mark 16:6 KJV). The women became the first of Jesus's supporters to know that He was resurrected. The Gospel of Mark said the women had reached a celestial world. To be sure, their vision was a revelation, and as with all revelations, it surprised with its newness and emotional potency.

In his depiction of Mary, Chilton argues that Mary was "one of the prime catalysts and shaping forces of Christianity." He calls out the New Testament Gospels for making only scattered references to her and sidelining her. Moreover, he says when the Gospels were written in the first century after Jesus's death, the scribes adhered to patriarchal Roman values in which men in families ruled over subservient women. This patriarchy stymied details about Mary's influence.

Yet Chilton, and many other scholars, recovered Mary's voice through study of the Gnostic Gospel, which existed along with New Testament Gospels in the first few hundred years after Jesus's death.

Gnostics have many interesting features. They believe that all people can have access to a loving and giving divinity. Barriers based on history or status are eschewed in favor of the idea that humans are all one in the presence of God and Jesus.

Mary was the consummate Gnostic. The authors of the religion allowed to her to emerge from her marginalization and be the revolutionary example she was. To be sure, her anointing skills and vision of a risen Christ made her the ideal spokeswoman for Christianity and its radical ideas about love and forgiveness.

The world needs to turn itself around due to human discord, and with the brave and good example of a loving Mary, that is possible.

Yearning for Relief: Seeing a Good Jesus for Christmas

Every Christmas, we laud the birth of Jesus Christ, and we embrace His majesty for helping the world.

The world is suffused with war and conflict, and one way to quell this desolate reality is to believe in Jesus Christ. To contemplate His splendor and understanding, we should begin by examining the story of His birth.

In his book *Desire of the Everlasting Hills: The World Before and After Jesus,* author Thomas Cahill presents the nativity story in a captivating manner.

The story is as follows:

Mary and Joseph were going to birth Jesus, the Messiah. Mary discovered her role in the Jesus narrative when she had a dream in which the angel Gabriel visited her. He told her she was good and that God favored her. He said she would bring Jesus into the world. He was the Son of God and would redeem the world. Mary chafed at the unreality of the dream but eventually relented and believed.

The actual place of Jesus's birth was in a room for livestock. Joseph's Bethlehem relatives were too poor for a more abundant place. Relieving this prison of poverty and spiritual oppression were to become essential parts of Jesus's ministry. Moreover, the birthplace challenges our current conceptions about the holiday. It should not be about giving material gifts. Instead, it should be about consoling the marginalized or anyone else who suffers. It should be a gift of empathy and restoration.

Jesus's eventual leadership was filled with His gentle countenance and empathy.

Jesus prodded believers toward the good news via His nature. As Cahill said, Jesus embraced listeners with an inclusive manner. He never condemned but encouraged. The Ten Commandments were not demanded but were calls for a benign dialogue. He came to save, not judge.

Jesus is known for His statements about turning the other cheek when faced with injustice. He is just as known for His tender care for the materially and spiritually oppressed.

Jesus's attention toward the poor and dispossessed is threaded throughout the New Testament. Some texts elucidate His generosity.

For instance, Jesus's last sermon before His crucifixion and resurrection was about hardship and the need to assuage it. It is among the most meaningful passages in all the scripture.

Jesus said the kingdom of God will welcome those who help: "For … I was thirsty and you gave me drink: I was stranger, and ye took me in: Naked and you clothed me," Jesus said. "I was sick, and ye visited me: I was in prison, and ye came unto me" (Matthew 25:35–36 KJV).

The love Jesus gives to the world is monumental and perennial. From studying Jesus, I have come to know what He believed in. He cared for the poor and innocent. He empathized with the lonely and gave shelter to the lost. He freed those in bondage. He was humble and sensitive.

We should care for Him as He cared for us. His message of consoling everyone who suffers touches believers across the world. Jesus's greatest message was to tell us that we are not alone in our dealings with struggle. That should relieve.

Jesus is within you. Make the future good and honest.

Part 4

Islam

Islamophobia and the American Experiment

Islamophobia is an exasperating issue that all Americans should care about.

In his new book, *Scapegoats*, human rights lawyer and public intellectual Arsalan Iftikhar has written a gorgeous elegy on the need for tolerance toward Muslims. Iftikhar's argument calls for acceptance of Muslims as an American necessity.

Islamophobia is a reality in our country and the world, and a large part of Iftikhar's book centers on defending his faith. He criticizes misunderstandings about Islam in the West and tries to educate the public about the true nature of his religion.

The Prophet Muhammad is the foundation of the Muslim faith. He is known for his trustworthiness and goodness, and from his revelations in the Quran, he guides Muslims toward a virtuous life.

Unfortunately, some in the west have hideously distorted his essence. In 2005, the Danish newspaper *Jylands-Posten* published derogatory cartoons that depicted the prophet as a dangerous and destructive villain. Later, some Muslim ambassadors sought a conversation with

Anders Fogh Rasmussen, the Danish prime minister, to ease the tensions surrounding the cartoons, but he refused. Because of this, global riots spread across the Muslim world.

Iftikhar condemned Muslim violence and also defended the Danish newspaper's right to publish the cartoons based on the principle of free speech. However, he also criticized the cartoons as malicious and damaging. "Just because something has the right to be published does not automatically mean that it should be deemed worthy of publication," he said.

Iftikhar portrayed the true essence of Muhammad as peaceful and full of love. He was not sinister as the Danish cartoon portrayed. To be sure, whenever he encountered antipathy, he did not seek retribution and largely turned the other cheek. Moreover, he was tolerant and judged people for their characters not their racial identities. As Muhammad said: "All mankind is from Adam and Eve; an Arab has no superiority over a non-Arab nor a non-Arab has any superiority over an Arab; also, a white has no superiority over black nor a black has any superiority over white except by piety and good action."

Sharia, or Islamic law, is another central facet of the Muslim faith. Sharia has existed for centuries and is a dialogue and interpretation of Muhammad's revelations in the Quran.

As with Muhammad, Sharia has been attacked and distorted by some in the West. Many conservatives have depicted Sharia as a danger to the American system. A majority of state legislatures have introduced anti-Sharia laws.

Yet the reality is entirely different. Iftikhar explains how Sharia is a diverse theology that is not bent on global domination. To be sure, as esteemed intellectual Leon Wieseltier points out, Sharia is akin to Halacha, or Jewish law, which Orthodox Jews follow. And while there are some Muslims who interpret Sharia in an oppressive manner, the bulk of it is replete with tolerance and love. As Harvard Law School professor Noah Feldman said, "(Sharia) is the most liberal and humane legal principles available anywhere in the world."

The ignorance and distortions surrounding Islam are dispiriting, and the current discourse in our country is distressing. Islamophobia has been simmering for over a decade and has fed the intolerance of politicians.

The invective has come from both the right and left. Christian leaders like Franklin Graham and Pat Robertson have called Islam evil and antithetical to peace. Meanwhile, liberal atheist Bill Maher said that Muslims are murderous and fretted about the Muslim fertility rate in the West.

Colin Powell has pushed back against this kind of Islamophobia. When right-wingers called President Obama a Muslim, he asserted that he was in fact a Christian. Yet he asked the imperative question of what is wrong with being a Muslim. The American answer is there's nothing wrong with it.

Making sure Muslims are treated equally in America is a daunting but crucial task. Yet America has dealt with scapegoating before. African Americans in addition to Jews and Catholics have been, and still are, denigrated in our country. These manacles of bigotry can be dismantled, and with bravery and fortitude, they can be defeated in the future.

Our country will inevitably know that Muslims are congruent with the best of America.

How Pluralism Might Solve Sectarian Violence in the Middle East

The fate of the Middle East is precarious, and America should help assuage war and promote human comity. We have a duty as leader of the free world to help mitigate escalating conflict.

With Donald Trump's national security team, he has an opportunity to fight extremism in the Middle East and promote societies that are pluralistic and ecumenical. In order to achieve this objective, he has to know the vicissitudes of religious sects, namely Sunnis and Shiites, and speak about sectarian peace.

To stem religious wars, one must understand how religion can be good or distorted. Religion can be a source of solace and meaning. Adherents can be guided by religion to live a life of virtue and moral direction. Yet when followers feel their religion is better than others and is the only route to divine truth, the result can be dismal.

While most Muslims are tolerant of different sects, some Sunnis and Shiite leaders and militant groups feel their religion is the supreme one. This intolerant certitude has ushered in violence. Muslim leaders at war need to respect diversity and freedom of religion as a good thing. To be sure, God doesn't discriminate among different religions. He cares for everyone.

In his book *Inside the Middle East*, former Israeli intelligence officer and educator Avi Melamed outlines the contours of these religious fights.

Sectarian violence has torn apart the Middle East, and Sunnis and Shiites are battling one another to the death. Sunni extremists like ISIS have disfigured the true meaning of Islam and have created an ideology enforced by violence and without regard to human decorum. Aside from terrorists, Sunni Saudi Arabia and its allies are fighting against Shiite Iran and its allies. The result has been a series of proxy wars between the two axes across the region.

The Sunni Shia split occurred after the Prophet Muhammad died in 632. The community of Muhamad's believers fought about who should lead them. The first leader was Abu Bakr, Muhammad's father-in-law. He was followed by Umar, another father-in-law, and then Uthman, a member of the powerful Umayyad dynasty. Ali, Muhammad's cousin and son-in-law, later led the community but was killed in 661.

The Sunnis believed the caliph should be appointed based on merit and theological education. The selection of Abu Bakr and then Umar and Uthmam reflected this belief. On the other side, the Shiites thought the caliph should be a direct descendant of Muhammad. Ali embodied this requirement.

From Iraq and Syria to Yemen and Israel, the Middle East has been riddled with violence. The most chaotic regions in terms of Sunni and Shiite violence have been in Iraq and Syria. In these regions, radical Islamic groups like ISIS, which are under the banner known as Salafi-Jihadis, have terrorized the region. Other Sunnis and Shiites have also contributed to the wars.

According to Melamed, the Salafi-Jihadi group believe in a very strict form of Sharia law. They want the emergence of a caliph immediately and want to overthrow existing Muslim political structures in order to implement their conservative Sharia beliefs. Moreover, they believe it is crucial to fight the West and Israel as they are seen to threaten Islam. All of these tenets are to be defended via violence. To be sure, the notion of martyrdom is lauded, and believers of this extreme ideology will fight to the death to achieve it.

The conditions that led to ISIS in Iraq occurred in 2014, over a decade after the initial American invasion in 2003. Iraq is a country with a Sunni majority and Shiite minority. In 2003, Saddam Hussein's reign ended, and he was killed in 2006. In his place to rule the country were Shiites Nuri al-Maliki and Haider al-Abadi. When he was leader of Iraq, Hussein, a Sunni, oppressed Shiites. Yet after Hussein was deposed and his army disbanded, Shiites, including Shiite militias from Iran, oppressed Sunnis. After the bulk of American troops left in 2011, fighting between Sunnis and Shias increased, wiping out some progress that had been achieved. In June 2014, Abu Bakr al-Baghdadi announced that he was caliph of ISIS.

ISIS's war efforts are gruesome. They flogged and beheaded anyone opposed to their rule. They have killed Christians and enslaved women and girls. Moreover, the Iraqi people have been atrociously persecuted. Hundreds of thousands have been killed and millions have been displaced.

The favorable news is that Iraq has routed ISIS, yet the country needs to work hard to restore their country. The country must encourage political representation of both Sunnis and Shia and promote economic vitality to rebuild the war-ravaged country. Moreover, they must offer humanitarian relief to dispossessed Iraqis. The demise of ISIS has been great for Iraq, yet they still suffer. To be sure, the traumatic injuries from ISIS's savagery need to heal.

ISIS has also ravaged Syria, which has a Sunni majority and Alawite Shiite minority. One of their most egregious crimes has been plundering ancient and sacred religious archeological sites. In May 2015, ISIS invaded the Syrian city of Palmyra, and they destroyed the Temples of Baalshamin and Baal. Their grotesque motive was to finance their war efforts and desecrate religions foreign to them.

Like Iraq, ISIS has been defeated in Syria, but the country is still rife with war from Sunni and Shia sects. On one side is a Sunni coalition of Saudi Arabia, Jordan, and Turkey. On the other side is Shiite Alawite Bashar al-Assad, the leader of Syria, and Iran, Hezbollah, Iraqi Shiite militias and Russia.

The current Syrian civil war began in January 2011 as a nonviolent uprising inspired by the Arab Spring. Armed with the internet and street protests, activists criticized the dictatorial regime of Bashar al-Assad and called for political reforms. Yet these noble efforts were eschewed when al-Assad responded militarily. There were stories of rape and killing of protesters. As a result, many Syrians abandoned the Syrian army and then cobbled together a rebel military force.

While the consensus in the West is that al-Assad must be removed, his backing by Iran, which has given him billions of dollars in aid, has propped him up. The result for the Syrian people has been disastrous. Half a million have been killed and millions have left their homes. There are many million refugees within Syria and many millions outside the country.

Melamed rues how perpetual war in the Middle East war masks real issues in the Arab world like poverty and lack of opportunity. Indeed, Melamed quoted Saudi journalist Abdulateef Al-Mulhim as saying that the real war in the Middle East is "corruption, lack of a good education, lack of good health care, lack of freedom, (and) lack of respect for the human lives."

The economic reality of the Middle East is crucial to understanding the rise of ISIS and the fervency of Arab Spring protestors. In terms of the former, disaffected Arabs living in countries with a lack of resources and a lack of social services feel powerless about their life circumstances, according to a May 2016 article in the *Guardian* newspaper. Leaders from groups like ISIS appeal to them with assertions that boost their self-worth, the article said.[3]

In terms of the latter, many Arab Spring protestors called for the improvement of economic conditions. In Egypt, one slogan called for bread, freedom, and social justice.

These realities lead to the importance of pluralism. It seems to me that one way to assuage sectarian violence is to have a democracy in which all groups are given a voice and treated equally. Free elections can transpire, and freedom of the press and freedom of religion will be guaranteed. If this is accomplished, people will have an impact on what their government chooses to work on. People could call for investments in the economy and things like education instead of endless war.

In the age of the internet in which people have a platform to air their opinions, the likelihood of achieving pluralism is increasingly possible. Rigid religious orthodoxy can be quelled, and individual empowerment can be attained. The Middle East is a beautiful region with an abundant history and customs, and there are many reasons for optimism and hope. Trump must educate himself about the region and encourage freedom and pluralism. Only then will peace be accomplished.

Choose Generosity, Not Exclusion: Thomas Jefferson and the Importance of Muslim Acceptance

America is place of paradoxes. It has undergone freedom and slavery and immigrant equality and xenophobia.

Donald Trump's travel ban barring refugees from Muslim countries from entering the United States was upheld by the Supreme Court in June 2018. The decision was abhorrent. It would not allow Muslims into our country from several countries, including Iran, Libya, Syria, Yemen, Somalia, Venezuela, and North Korea. The ruling flouted American pluralistic values and instead appealed to a darker nativist past where fear and prejudice was rampant. It rejects and torments those seeking a better life in our country.

The ban was first proposed in January 2017, and different versions of it winnowed its way through challenges in the courts.

The original January 2017 version of the ban created panic. Throngs of protesters gathered at airports bearing signs decrying Trump and welcoming refugees. Lawyers with laptops were present to offer legal advice to those affected by the ban. While the protests were thrillingly heartfelt, they were also chaotic and frightening. The raw emotion reflected the speed and lack of thought that went into the order.

The bottom line for America is that we should ponder American principles and fight in Congress to overturn the decision. At its best, America offers refuge for those afflicted with hardship across the world. As the inscription on the Statue of Library reads: "America offers your tired, your poor, your huddled masses yearning to be free, the wretched refuse by your teeming shore. Send these, the tempest-tost to me." Congressman Keith Ellison put it more succinctly when writing about Islamophobia generally: "Choose Generosity, Not Exclusion."

One way to contemplate American values is to heed the example of Thomas Jefferson. In her magisterial book, *Thomas Jefferson's Quran*, writer Denise Spellberg creates a comprehensive portrait of how Jefferson helped establish our country's ideal of pluralism generally and for Muslims in particular. He created a principle that fought discrimination.

The argument for Muslim equality has a theological feature, and Jefferson subscribed to it. Muslims believe in parts of the Hebrew scripture and the New Testament, and thus it can be argued that they, along with Jews and Christians, worship the same God. Jefferson concurred. A Deist and Unitarian, he believed in a unitary and universal God.

Yet what mattered most to Jefferson was not the rightness of his religion, but the acceptance of all religions, an ideal he promulgated in the legal and political spheres of early America. He thought that he, along with people of every religious stripe, deserved to be able to follow his conscience without coercion from the state.

Jefferson was a warrior for religious equality, yet he was a product of his time, believing that Islam was an oppressive religion. This kind of Islamophobia was extensive in Europe and spilled across the

Atlantic into America. It was rooted in the 1500s rhetoric of Protestant reformers like Martin Luther and John Calvin, who said Catholicism and Islam represented the anti-Christ. Later, in the late 1600s, Englishman Humphrey Prideaux wrote a polemic that said that the Prophet Muhammad was an imposter. Early Americans like Cotton Mather and Anne Hutchinson shared these views, and then in various iterations, they persisted through Jefferson's day and beyond to today.

Jefferson's excursion toward pluralism and Islam's place in this concept began in 1765, when he bought a Quran from George Sale. Sale thought the Quran was an offshoot of the Hebrew scriptures and the New Testament, and he respected the religion's piety and morality. Simultaneously, he felt Muslims should convert to Christianity.

Jefferson began to study religious freedom and Islam in the mid-1760s. He poured over seventeenth-century British legal precedents, and he authored *Literary and Legal Commonplace Books*. The notes said that Muslims, along with Jews, were not enemies of the British crown.

This small piece of opinion blossomed into Jefferson's meaningful 1777 legislation for the Commonwealth of Virginia: a bill for establishing religious freedom. Passed in 1786, Jefferson said the bill, along with the Declaration of Independence and the creation of the University of Virginia, were his proudest achievements.

The bill was revolutionary as it drew on past European polemics tolerating Muslims within a Christian polity to become a directive that proclaimed universal religious freedom in a pluralistic nation.

The differences occurred in the following manner:

One of the European thinkers who inspired Jefferson was John Locke. In his 1689 polemic *A Letter Concerning Toleration*, Locke called for civil rights for non-Christians. Jefferson quoted Locke writing: "(He) sais 'neither Pagan nor Mahamedan nor Jew ought to be excluded from the civil rights of the Commonwealth because of his religion."

Jefferson went further than Locke, saying that civil rights were imperative but that every religion was equal. In contrast, Locke believed in Christian superiority, and he felt, like Sale, that salvation for non-Christians could only be achieved via conversion.

The distinction between Locke and Jefferson was a microcosm of the religious debate at large. Many Americans at the time felt that Protestantism should be the dominant religion. As an example, many felt that a religious test for Protestantism was needed if a citizen wanted to hold public office. While this was outlawed in the US Constitution, which was ratified in 1788, the rift about the issue was real.

To be sure, in the 1800 election for president, Jefferson was submitted to a de facto religious test. Jefferson's opponents depicted him as a Muslim and were afraid of his message of universal religious freedom. As Spellberg said, "The basic strategy was to play on the perception that America was a Christian nation and that the danger of a non-Christian president was imminent in Jefferson."

The watershed actions by Jefferson should be a guide for our new-century America. Those distressed by the Muslim ban must vote. Then Congress should propose legislation to counter the Supreme Court decision. America should defend our diverse nation and accept Muslims. The issue is too important for inaction.

Part 5

Ecumenism and America

Humane and Savage:
A Novel Reflects
Nineteenth-Century Pursuits

The New Bedford Samurai, a novel recently written by Anca Vlasopolos, a professor and director of comparative literature at Wayne State University, is a beautiful rendering of economic pursuit and binding humane relationships during the nineteenth century.

Part coming-of-age story, part life biography, the story centers on a Japanese man named Manjiro Nakahama, who was shipwrecked as a boy on an uninhabited island and rescued by an American whaling captain named William Whitfield. Whitfield took Nakahama and his Japanese compatriots on board his ship and subsequently chose Nakahama to be his protégé and quasison. He vowed to teach Nakahama the English language and the vicissitudes of whaling. After many years of instruction in American manners, Nakahama grew into an educated young man with a good and honest character. He went on to a full life of material and emotional success.

Nakahama's story was influenced by both the great and boundless economic opportunity and freedom engendered in America in addition to the sometime ugly components of our country's history, namely discrimination toward nonwhites and an excessive reaching for profit that can result in environmental degradation.

Vlasopolos's description of Nakahama's immersion in the American economy is vivid and entrancing. The opportunities before him required hard work and a stamina for staving off danger. Despite the possibilities of failure, Nakahama and most of his fellow seamen prospered. Nakahama made successful whaling journeys and wrested a fair amount of money from participating in the California gold rush.

Nakahama's economic success hinged on the love and attention Whitfield gave to him during his first years with him. He nurtured Nakahama and showed him the difference between right and wrong.

One anecdote reveals how Whitfield inculcated tolerant and accepting values in Nakahama. After Nakahama attended church with Whitfield, the reverend of the church told Whitfield that Nakahama must sit in the back pews because of his color. Incensed, Whitfield told the reverend that he was a free soiler, a precursor of Lincoln's Republican Party that embraced work and opportunity for everyone. Nakahama should be accepted regardless of his race, he felt.

Later, Whitfield talked with Nakahama about the incident and expressed his beliefs in decency for humans at large as well as for Nakahama.

"God works in mysterious ways. This is an opportunity for me, for us, to find true Christian enlightenment among our fellows," Whitfield said. "I've long believed in certain things. Ideas such as justice, compassion and a measure of fair play."

Thus, when Nakahama was bombarded with epithets from students at his school and during his travels in the West, he calmly endured them. Whitfield showed him they were wrong, and in the process, Nakahama was confident about who he became.

When met with greed and savagery while at sea, Nakahama searched his soul and asked whether there was a downside to the American economy. When he was first aboard Whitfield's boat, he witnessed a whale hunt and shuddered at its mercilessness. He pondered the frightening similarities between the hunters and the hunted. The violence of the pursuit resembled the violence of the pursued.

In another event he witnessed a mutiny after a captain went insane, foaming at the mouth and disrespecting his fellow seaman and nature.

Many years after the mutiny, during his adulthood when he was a captain on a voyage, he encountered two men who sought to raid his ship. Nakahama made one of them his prisoner. He subsequently questioned whether he was like the captain on the mutinous ship.

"How could he have let anger get the better of him, of him who had worked so hard toward reasoned understanding among men," he thought.

Nakahama's thoughts about the savagery of whaling can be seen as a harbinger for future environmentalists in the twentieth century. Like current preservers of our planet, he saw how an unbridled search for profit in whaling must be checked in order to protect nature and one another.

Yet there are limits in Nakahama's thoughts toward the environment. At the end of the novel, Vlasopolos wrote about the albatross bird as it relates to Nakahama. Nearing the end of his life when he went back to Japan, Nakahama prodded a friend to hunt the albatross in order to sell its feathers abroad in Europe and America.

Nakahama was cognizant about the need to nurture the planet, and he considered the bird's welfare. However, he didn't have the example of the environmental movement to foresee the long-term problems that might surface by hunting the bird. Indeed, the bird became virtually extinct until the late twentieth century, when it was protected and nurtured to a sustainable level by a Japanese ornithologist.

Perhaps Vlasopolos included the albatross account to suggest that good people like Nakahama have the potential to be protectors of the world if they are equipped with knowledge and awareness. By giving attention to the dear nature of the environment, we can all save the world if we have commitment and care. The end of the novel thus serves as a beginning.

Cobbled together through research and a vast imagination on the part of Vlasopolos, Nakahma's story inspires and engages. Vlasopolos's values, realized through her description and penchant for Nakahama, seep through the text. She embraces American freedom and economic opportunity but argues for a consciousness about its excesses.

The novel, marvelously written and marvelous in its arc, captivates with its reverence for nature and humans.

The Flavors of Faith Helps Religious Communities Grow

I recently went to an interfaith meeting at the Beth Shalom synagogue in Oak Park, Michigan, and met Lynne Meredith Golodner, a longtime food writer. Golodner has just published a tremendous book dubbed *The Flavors of Faith* about the nexus between religion and bread.

The book is beautifully written, and with bread as its fulcrum, it explores essential ideas about God, community, love, and human comity.

Examining the religion of various faith groups, Golodner shows how sharing bread with others in a religious setting can create progress. God love coupled with fellow human love spurs human and communal growth. No matter what religion or culture, bread is a unifier in the quest for religious morality.

Golodner begins her book with a history of bread. Humans made flatbreads twelve thousand years ago. The Greeks followed by nurturing fifty types of bread. The Romans then instituted the concept of a public bakery. In terms of the predominate religious groups Golodner looks at, including Native American, Jewish, Christian, and Islam, bread is important for each faith.

The breads Golodner documents come in every shape, flavor, and density, said David Crumm, editor of *ReadtheSpirit,* the magazine that has published *The Flavors of Faith.* They are round, braided, and oblong. They are spicy and syrupy. They have a crisp quality and alternately a soft one.

Golodner dashes a panoply of recipes throughout her book from each religion she explores. Included is a tantalizing coconut cake recipe by the poet Emily Dickinson, a Jewish challah bread creation, a Native American corn bread recipe authored by chef Annabel Cohen, a bread dough concocted by local Muslim women, and a St. Joseph's Christian altar bread amalgam.

In the religions she chose, Golodner looks carefully at the relationship between God and bread.

Her description of Native American religion enthralls. Native American religion is not part of the Abrahamic tradition, which includes Judaism, Christianity, and Islam, yet it has a complex and meaningful divinity within its cultural tradition.

The conflation of Native American bread and spirituality mirrors the community's experience of adversity and optimism. Many Native Americans like eating a concoction called fry bread. Yet its ingredients are not made in the Americas, and it is associated with colonization and oppression, Golodner said. In contrast, Golodner praises corn bread, made out of maize, and other bread ingredients like maple syrup and pecans. These latter ingredients are grown within Native American communities and thus connote a sense of respect and communal solidarity.

In the Abrahamic religions, Judaism, Christianity, and Islam, the notion of a covenant with God and a covenant within a community is paramount. While Golodner doesn't delve into the theology of scripture, she brilliantly describes how bread in all these religions underscores respect for God and one another.

Challah bread, a soft, doughy creation, is suffused throughout Judaism. Jews eat challah every Saturday for the Sabbath, the Jewish day of rest. Additionally, they eat it at many holidays. The most significant use of challah in the Jewish tradition is the adaption of it for the central and meaningful holiday of Passover. As described in the Torah book of Exodus, Jews led by Moses were in such a hurry to flee Egypt and the bondage they endured there that they left before their bread had risen. Thus, in memory of this event, Jews eat unleavened challah bread called matzah during Passover.

Bread and Christianity have been intertwined since the days of Jesus. At the Last Supper, Jesus offered bread and wine to His disciples as a symbol of His body and blood. Named communion, Jesus desired this process for Christians so that they can reflect Jesus's love.

The permutations among different Christian sects about the role of bread is vast. Just looking at the employment of unleavened versus leavened bread, many interpretations abound. For some Catholic Christians, unleavened bread is the most favorable manner to salvation and goodness. To be sure, this type of bread was eaten in the Jewish temple and at the Last Supper. Renowned Catholic priest Father Dan Merz said in Golodner's book that leavened bread has been an ominous symbol of deterioration. By eating unleavened bread, believers could wait for God's help and start over, he said.

"[U]nleavened bread includes that symbolism of inactivity so that God can come and act on us. His power can be manifest," Merz said.

Simultaneously, Protestant Christians see leavened bread as benign and eat it during communion. Merz says it is not a debate about right or wrong but a divergence in custom. To be sure, while Jesus and His disciples ate unleavened bread during the Last Supper, Jesus also refers to leavened bread in a good manner, namely as a symbol of the kingdom of God.

In the most recent Abrahamic religion, Islam, bread is a significant part of Muslims' lives. At the Islamic Center of America in Dearborn, Michigan, women bake spicy bread continuously. Muslim women bake the bread for the sustenance of its members. Some members buy the bread to send to relatives across the country. Because the mosque does not have dues or a tithe, the women's bread baking is a fundamental process for making revenue.

"They are the backbone of the ICA," said Imam Hassan Qazwini, the leader of the mosque. "If it wasn't for them, maybe we couldn't have made it so far."

While the Quran only mentions bread once in the story of Joseph, the idea of feeding the poor is vociferously sprinkled throughout the Holy Book. Imam Qazwini relayed a story by the prophet Muhammad to Golodner that elucidates God's advocacy for giving the needy sustenance.

A man named Ibrahim was known for hosting and feeding strangers in his house. So when he was having meal with a stranger and asked to commune in prayer, the guest said, "'Pray to who?'" Incensed, Ibrahim rescinded his offer to feed him. But then God sent the angel Gabriel to Ibrahim and castigated him. Ibrahim apologized.

The meaning of the story was, as Golodner summarized from the imam, that "Muslims believe that God's generosity must be extended to the world by believers who will help to feed others in need."

Another example of the primacy of giving food to the needy in Islam occurs during the holy month of Ramadan. By fasting, Muslims get to know what it is like to be hungry, and thus they are more likely to give to those who need food, the imam explained.

Golodner's book strikingly portrays how members of major religions create and share bread in order to praise God and human creation. Bread can help humans and faith groups advance and exhibit love.

The Case for Miracles

Miracles can make change conceivable.

In his book *Miracles*, author Eric Metaxas makes the case for why they are so important for our present human condition and how they have happened since the creation of Earth.

Miracles appear in small and large ways. They heal illnesses and broken hearts. They can guide the shape of history. They can change hearts and minds. They renew our sense of wonder with God's loving omnipotence and omniscience.

Metaxas is very poised to write a book on miracles. His work has been largely about humans who have worked for change with tremendous empathy and conviction. To be sure, he has written books about William Wilberforce and Dietrich Bonheoffer, who stood up for enslaved Africans and persecuted Jews respectively. The tales of these men that Metaxas wrote about are a type of miracle: they transformed the world in a very humane way.

A Christian, Metaxas cites events in human history that can only be seen as miracles, and he convincingly argues that God is the source of them. He describes the parting of the Red Sea, the virgin birth of Jesus, Jesus's resurrection, and Jesus's miracles like healing the blind and maimed. While he did not mention it, the night journey in Islam in which the Prophet Muhammad met other prophets and ascended into heaven before traveling back to Earth can also be seen as a miracle.

Metaxas's basic thesis is that God, outside the earth's closed system of scientific laws, reaches into earth with miracles to lovingly communicate with humans and help them thrive and survive.

"He sees what we are going through and he cares," Metaxas writes. "Furthermore, he is such a big God that he can afford to deal with us on an intimate level, to encourage us and to hold our hands."

Metaxas delineates the philosophy and theology of miracles with insight and panache. He describes how science and God are not mutually exclusive but actually splendidly compatible. An example is the creation of the Earth, which Metaxas says could only have happened with God's prodding.

Scientific research has established the big bang theory of how Earth was made, Metaxas said. A planet larger than Mars speeding to a destination for millions of years collided with Earth in a very precise manner that made life and humans possible. When it collided, chunks of matter began orbiting Earth and became the moon. The moon, whose luminous beauty all humans can savor, also guides the ebb and flows of the sea in addition to stabilizing the earth's axis. In Metaxas's opinion, the exactitude of the collision was not random but was most likely orchestrated by an essence outside the universe, most likely by God.

Metaxas's opinions cohere with the reality that many scientists came to faith via scientific study. He says that the invention of modern science was created from some scientists who were also Christian. They believed that theology and science were inextricably linked.

Although he was not a Christian, Einstein said the search for scientific meaning is animated by a divine spirituality.

"Everyone who is seriously involved in the pursuit of science becomes convinced that a spirit is manifest in the laws of the Universe—a spirit vastly superior to that of man, and one of which we with our modest powers must feel humble," he said.

Metaxas also wrestles with the question of why some prayers do not result in miracles. He says God loves humans beyond measure and is with humans in the long run. For instance, Metaxas says God may allow suffering because He knows its existence could eventually lead to meaning and redemption.

Metaxas describes some examples of this process. John Newton, the author of the song "Amazing Grace," jettisoned his involvement in the slave trade because he realized it was morally unjust and repellent. His repentant journey to becoming a Christian preacher was hard but eventually morally correct and satisfying.

"I have reasons to praise (God) for my trials, for, most probably, I should have been ruined without them," he said.

Belief in God's miracles can bolster the fragile human spirit. War between humans and countries often stem from harboring past grievances. Humans must find their humane hearts and forgive one another. Via miracles, change can happen: broken hearts can heal and wars can end. Please pray for the miracles of love, peace, honesty, and change. A life-giving God would be elated.

Naming a Religion: The Spiritual Beliefs of Native Americans

The religious identity of a culture delineates what it deems meaningful, and this is particularly true for Native Americans.

To understand Native American religion, one should begin with Sam Gill's *Native American Religions: An Introduction.*

Gill imparts how Native America religion speaks to all facets of life. It orders the cosmos and the earth via life-giving rituals that define for Native Americans who they are.

Naming an individual in Native American cultures is paramount as it gives a person an identity. The process of naming mirrors the practice of religion at large. Just as naming locates a person in a community, the transmission of religious rituals and stories locate a community's religious identity.

Naming is associated with ceremonies and rituals. Children receive names as soon as they emerge from a mother's womb. He or she is usually named after an esteemed elder or ancestor. Names are also given for different ages in life. A name is important as it reflects the soul and thus the very essence of life and being.

The Navajo spiritual life can be named by delving into its characteristics. Healing is one example. People who are sick find treatment via sand painting. The works are painted on the floor of a home and depict holy people whose presence can heal. The patient goes to the middle of the painting, where he or she becomes identified with the holy people. Illnesses then diminish. At the end of the rite, sand in the painting is scattered back to Mother Earth. Just as sand returns to its home in the environment, so do once ailing Navajos return to a home of good physical health with feelings of rootedness.

One of the most astounding features of Native American religion is its survival and longevity amid European and American Christians stealing their land and sometimes trying to convert them to Christianity by force.

While there are numerous examples of European and American fair treatment toward Native Americans, their loss and tears seem more prevalent. Native American spirituality is just as vast and imperative as Christianity, yet the group still feels the burden of physical and moral displacement.

In order to remedy the injustices against them, Americans should study their history and, most importantly, their abundant religious history. The value of such an endeavor will both enrich students about a complex and appealing set of beliefs and give Native Americans their due as a culture worthy of respect and affection.

President John F. Kennedy voiced this idea about how knowledge of Native American history can restore and buttress their dignity.

"Only through this study can we as a nation do what must be done if our treatment of the American Indians is not to be marked down for all time as a national disgrace," he said.

We should all exhibit grace to Native Americans by respecting their forever-stirring religion and way of life. Their names matter.

A Thoughtful Gem: David McCullough on the American Spirit

American history is one of the most splendid stories ever told, and in his book *The American Spirit*, historian David McCullough outlines its soul beautifully.

For McCullough, history is essential because it tells us who we are and what we stand for. Since its inception, each generation has imbibed American history as a way to laud the past and navigate the future. From things like the Declaration of Independence to the Bill of Rights and environmental safeguards, American leaders and movements have created a country defined by freedom and human decorum. Its illustrious contours resonate today and prompt Americans to proceed honorably and with insight.

In addition to being a great writer, McCullough is a great teacher, and he embraces education on America as a conduit for human understanding and action. He lauds teachers as people who love their profession and impact students in a life-transforming manner. Learning about race comes to my mind. Studying the history of African Americans will nurture tolerance and effect change in movements like Black Lives Matter, I think.

McCullough's book comprises speeches he has given at universities and on American anniversaries. Often, he gives histories of past leaders and events at each location. In particular, he explores great leaders and politicians who made a difference by their exemplary character and political fortitude.

One such leader was Marquis de Lafayette. He was from France and served as a general in the Continental Army during the Revolutionary War. His bravery in war made him a symbol of American heroism. In 1824, he enthusiastically returned to America from France and went on a twenty-four-state tour, where he met leaders and explored the sacred sites of our country and regional natural wonders. He encountered jubilant crowds and parades.

Lafayette can be seen as a microcosm for the good and lasting peace and cooperation we have with France. While Americans and France were on opposite sides during the French and Indian War, our relationship since then has been productive. It began with the eighteenth-century Treaty of Paris that declared the end of the Revolutionary War, and it has flourished through centuries.

To be sure, France and America fought side by side in World Wars I and II. Many American artists lived in France during this time, inspired by artistic institutions like the Louvre. Some included Edith Wharton and William Faulkner. Moreover, France bequeathed us the Statue of Liberty, and French civil engineers helped create the Brooklyn Bridge.

Conjuring today, America has given reassurance and solace to France when they have endured terrorist attacks.

President John F. Kennedy was another American hero. An icon of grace and charm, he worked on equal opportunity in addition to service and the primacy of hearts and minds. Moreover, his speech was poetry.

"He spoke to the point and with confidence. He knew words matter," McCullough said. "His words changed lives. His words changed history. Rarely has a commander-in-chief addressed the nation with such a command of language."

This oratory has moved many to work in public service, it seems to me. One can think of some of his accomplishments like the Peace Corps and the fight against Communism as harbingers for the brave leaders who followed him in their work for world peace and American democratic and capitalistic values.

McCullough's love of American leaders extends to the process of government action and the life of public discourse.

America is rooted in ideals of freedom from the founders to Abraham Lincoln and Kennedy. Leaders are purely American when they both speak their values and allow dissent. They are American when they find common ground or have new ideas. Freedom can take many forms, and thus it is imperative that the dialogue is open and not stifled on either side of the aisle. To be sure, as far as Kennedy thought, Americans should treat one another in the way they wanted to be treated.

With our nation embattled in rancor, it is important to see what is meaningful in the world.

We, said Kennedy, "will be remembered not for our victories or defeats in battle or in politics, but for our contributions to the human spirit."

We hope for our military to prevail in the world. Simultaneously, we should look to history to find transcendence and salvation for our national spirit.

The Increasing Care of Bobby Kennedy

America needs leaders who can soothe our national soul and change things for the better. There are many areas where we can make progress. Some include trying to compromise on health-care legislation to ensure most Americans are covered to healing the ravaging opioid epidemic that has claimed the lives of hundreds of thousands of Americans.

How do we find leaders that will placate our spirit and find solutions to issues afflicting our polity? We should look to the life of Bobby Kennedy.

Enter Chris Matthews. Matthews, a good and honest journalist, has written a masterful biography on the good and honest politician Bobby Kennedy. It is called *Bobby Kennedy: A Raging Spirit.*

Bobby is the kind of leader current leaders should emulate. He inspired and captivated. The crux of his soulful mission was to help others no matter what their life circumstances.

For Matthews, the killing of Jack Kennedy made a before and after moment for him. So it was for Bobby too. To be sure, the book delineates the course of Bobby's life during Jack's life and after it. He went from being tough and adamant against immorality to being close and understanding toward Americans in peril in the shadows of our country.

At the end of Matthews' book, he describes the train ride bearing a deceased Bobby from New York to Washington, DC's Union Station. Millions of Americans from all walks of life chanted "God bless you," and "We love you, Bobby." In Philadelphia, a group of mostly African Americans sang "Battle Hymn of the Republic."

The flood of sorrow and care toward Bobby was important for our country. It revealed the pathos-driven, empathetic leader that Bobby had become, Matthews said.

"He was, for so many, the one American leader of our lives who refused to turn his eyes from the people swept aside," Matthews said.

To understand how he became such a great icon—and to see how his example should be heeded today—Americans must pour through the vicissitudes of his life in order to see his goodness and altruism.

Bobby and Jack were inextricably joined. While Jack was elegant and sociable and Bobby awkward and quiet, they still made a good team. To be sure, Bobby became obdurate in both safeguarding Jack and helping him get elected in both his senate and presidential runs. Moreover, he served as Jack's attorney general.

The civil rights movement is essential for understanding America in the Kennedy years, and Jack and Bobby were on the right side of history by opposing injustice and oppression toward African Americans. Bobby, unwavering and resolute, was responsible for challenging the racist system on the ground, while Jack used his role as president to speak against it.

In May 1961, Bobby was confronted with helping freedom riders, a group of civil rights activists who were protesting Jim Crow by driving across the Deep South. Though he favored the role of courts in achieving racial justice versus civil obedience, Bobby cared about the riders. To be sure, he was aghast when they were beaten and their buses firebombed. When he heard about another group riding, he dispatched his aide John Siegenthaler to convince them to desist. They refused, and he then followed them only to be beaten himself. This incident made Bobby aware of the seriousness of the violence and racial vitriol. He knew there must be change.

Later, in April 1963, Bobby made real progress to end racial oppression. Martin Luther King Jr. decided to fight Jim Crow by leading marches in Birmingham, Alabama. As they walked, throngs of protestors were beaten and endured Public Safety Commissioner Eugene Connor's spraying of firehoses at them. Bobby called on Burke Marshall, head of the Justice Department's Civil Rights Division, to mediate the dispute between business leaders and civil rights activists. Burke achieved most of the protesters demands, namely no signs separating whites and blacks in addition to desegregation of lunch counters and help with improving African American employment.

From his work, Bobby convinced Jack to make a civil rights speech. He had arguments for the cause because he viscerally felt the anguish of civil rights movement activists and the injustice of their white tormentors.

Jack delivered with a heartfelt and moving speech that appealed to Americans' consciences amid the grave racial strife.

He spoke: "One hundred years of delay have passed since President Lincoln's freed slaves, yet their heirs, their grandsons, are not fully free. They are not yet freed from social and economic oppression. And this Nation, for all its hopes and boasts, will not be fully free until its citizens are free."

When Jack was killed in November 1963, Bobby was devastated. He had worshipped and devoted his life to Jack. As one aide said, Jack's death made Bobby a brooder, one "who carried the agony of the world."

What is commendable about Bobby is how he transformed his suffering into increasing care for the marginalized. He was distressed by Americans who were dispossessed and seemingly forgotten.

Matthews described some things he worried about: "The children of the Mississippi Delta with their distended stomachs and 'destroyed minds,' the Indians living on reservations where the most common cause of death is suicide, of the impoverished whites in Appalachia and the families in the black ghettos of the big cities. In each case, he pronounced the conditions 'unacceptable.'"

Bobby's empathy for the poor and African Americans were some particular areas that revealed his intensifying empathy for the downtrodden.

Having heard about the overwhelming poverty in the Mississippi Delta, Bobby went to the region himself in April 1967 to corroborate the dire conditions. Families suffered from lack of food and shoddy living conditions. He went to one house where roaches were everywhere. He saw a malnourished boy with sores on his body playing on a dirty floor. Bobby touched the boy's cheek and said: "My God, I didn't know this kind of thing existed! Maybe they just don't know." He then began to cry.

Bobby wanted to disseminate the atrocious conditions in order to institute reforms. He had human rights activist and child psychiatrist Robert Coles testify about the effects of poverty on families. By the 1970s, conditions improved via government and political action group efforts.

Coles was moved by Bobby's care for the impoverished. He knew "vulnerability alongside privilege and power" and had a "willingness to put himself in the shoes of others, as well as walking in his own."

Race is another area where Bobby deepened his empathy. While Bobby's toughness was needed to combat Jim Crow in the early 1960s, after Jack's death, he was melancholy albeit still fervent about race. He promulgated his empathy in many speeches.

One such speech was in South Africa. Bobby spoke of the similarities of America and South Africa. Having some success at ending Jim Crow, he then sought to provide meaning about why racial justice is important.

"They are differing evils; but they are common works of man. They reflect the imperfections of human justice, the inadequacy of human compassion," he said about the countries. "And therefore, they call upon common qualities of conscience and indignation, a shared determination to wipe away the unnecessary sufferings of fellow human beings at home and around the world."

Bobby was shattered upon hearing of the killing of Martin Luther King Jr. He gave an incredibly inspiring speech in Indianapolis to a largely African American crowd following the news of King's death. As Jack had been killed, Bobby told the crowd he identified with their sorrow and anger. But he said hatred is not the right response. Bobby had eschewed his skepticism about civil disobedience and supported it.

He spoke:

> For those of you were black—considering the evidence evidently is that there were white people who were responsible—you can be filled with bitterness, and with hatred, and a desire for revenge. We can move in that direction as a country, in a great

polarization—black people amongst black, and white amongst white, filled with hatred toward one another.

"Or we can make an effort, as Martin Luther King did, to understand and to comprehend and replace that violence," he went on, "with an effort to understand compassion and love."

The killing of Bobby in June 1968 was a violent national calamity. His death shook the American soul. He had become an icon of anguish and empathy, and his death swallowed his humane efforts.

Yet Bobby's spirit is not dead. His example lives on to help humans to reach for goodness and peace and love for one another. We should all board an American train headed for salvation and human transcendence. Bobby, like all of us, would be enthralled.

Bibliography

Part 1: Race

Braude, Ann. *Sisters and Saints: Women and American Religion*. New York: Oxford, 2008.

Foner, Eric. *Forever Free: The Story of Emancipation and Reconstruction*. New York: Knopf, 2005.

Goodwin, Doris Kearns. *Team of Rivals: The Political Genius of Abraham Lincoln*. New York: Simon & Schuster, 2000.

Jones, Jaqueline. *Labor of Love, Labor of Sorrow: Black Women and the Family from Slavery to the Present*. New York: Basic Books, 2010.

Lewis, John. *Across that Bridge: Life Lessons and a Vision for Change*. New York: Hyperion, 2012.

Morrison, Toni. *What Moves at the Margin*. Jackson: University Press of Mississippi, 2008.

Spencer, Chauncey. *Who Is Chauncey Spencer?* Detroit: Broadside Press, 1975.

Tutu, Desmond and Mpho. *Made for Goodness*. New York: Harper Collins, 2011.

Part 2: Judaism

Frankl, Viktor. *Man's Search for Meaning*. Boston: Beacon Press, 2017.

Milgrom, Jeremy. "Let Your Love for Me Vanquish Your Hatred: Nonviolence and Modern Judaism." In *Subverting Hatred: The Challenge of Nonviolence in Religious Traditions*, edited by Daniel L. Smith-Christopher. New York: Orbis Books, 2007.

Naim, Asher. *Saving a Lost Tribe: The Rescue and Redemption of the Ethiopia Jews*. New York, NY: Ballantine Books, 2003.

Styron, William. *My Generation: Collective Nonfiction*. New York: Random House, 2015.

Part 3: Christianity

Cahill, Thomas. *Desire of the Everlasting Hills: The World Before and After Jesus*. New York: Nan A. Talese, 1999.

Cone, James. *God of the Oppressed*. New York: Seabury Press, 1975.

Chilton, Bruce. *Mary Magdalene: A Biography*. New York: Doubleday, 2005.

Francis, Pope. *Church of Mercy: A Vision for the Church*. Chicago: Loyola, Jesuit Ministry, 2014.

Japinga, Lynn. *Feminism and Christianity: An Essential Guide*. Nashville: Abingdon Press, 1999.

Part 4: Islam

Iftikhar, Arsalan. *Scapegoats: How Islamophobia Helps Our Enemies and Threatens Our Freedoms*. New York: Skyhorse Publishing, 2017.

Melamed, Avi. *Inside the Middle East: Making Sense of the Most Dangerous and Complicated Region on Earth.* New York: Skyhorse Publishing, 2016.

Spellberg, Denise. *Thomas Jefferson's Quran: Islam and the Founders.* New York: Penguin Random House, 2013.

Part 5: Ecumenism and America

Gill, Sam. *Native American Religions: An Introduction.* Belmont: Wadsworth Publishing, 2004.

Golodner, Lynn Meredith. *The Flavors of Faith.* Ann Arbor: Front Edge Publishing, 2013.

McCullough, David. *The American Spirit: Who We Are and What We Stand For.* New York: Simon & Schuster, 2017.

Matthews, Chris. *Bobby Kennedy: A Raging Spirit.* New York: Simon & Schuster. 2017.

Metaxas, Eric. *Miracles: What They Are, Why They Happen, and How They Can Change Your Life.* New York: Dutton Penguin Group, 2014.

Vlasopolos, Anca. *The New Bedford Samurai.* Kingsport: Twilight Times Books, 2007.

Endnotes

1   Carlo Strenger, "Talking Cure Diplomacy," *New York Times*, 26 May 2010.

2   Tallie Lipkin-Shahak, "Nabka Day May 2001," *Jerusalem Post*, 19 June 2001.

3   Ian Black, "How Poverty Is Driving Syrian Men and Boys into the Arms of Isis," *The Guardian*, 4 May 2016.

Printed in the United States
By Bookmasters